O'NEILL: CREST OF A WAVE

O'NEILL: CREST OF A WAVE
THE FIRST TWO YEARS

by
GEOFF PETERS

First published 1998

**First published in Great Britain in 1998
by Kingmar Publishing and Geoff Peters.**

ISBN 0 9532849 0 5

A CIP catalogue record for this book is available from the British Library.

Designed by Geoff Peters in association with Martin Reeves and David Snell of Printstream Limited.

Printed and typeset by Printstream Limited,
33 Ashville Way, Whetstone, Leicester LE8 6NU.
Tel: 0116 275 0057

CONTENTS

PART ONE:

PART TWO:

ACKNOWLEDGMENTS

THERE ARE A NUMBER OF PEOPLE AND ORGANISATIONS WHO I WOULD LIKE TO THANK FOR THEIR HELP - WHETHER LARGE OR SMALL - IN GETTING THIS BOOK INTO YOUR HANDS. HERE ARE A FEW, IN NO PARTICULAR ORDER.

Nick Carter, Editor of the *Leicester Mercury*
Gary Silke, Editor of *The Fox* fanzine
Kevin Bourgault, printing maestro
Dave Morcom, photographer to the stars
Russ Carvell, great cartoonist
Printstream, Whetstone
Kingmar Publishing
Paramore-Heronway Marketing & Distribution
Andy, the Elizabethan Restaurant, Welford
Leicestershire Record Office, Wigston
Kevin and the team @ Barclays Bank.

SOME INFORMATION REPRODUCED IN THIS BOOK APPEARS BY KIND PERMISSION OF THE *LEICESTER MERCURY*, AND *THE FOX* FANZINE. PICTURES APPEAR COURTESY OF DAVE MORCOM PHOTOGRAPHY. I WOULD ALSO LIKE TO THANK RUSS CARVELL, WHO OWNS THE COPYRIGHT TO ALL THE CARICATURES IN THIS BOOK.

ABOUT THE AUTHOR

BORN in Leicestershire in the early 1970s, Geoff Peters came into this world armed with a microphone and notebook. Although his parents Henry and Jean, and older sister Diane didn't realise it then, Geoff was to become the BBC's youngest ever local radio Sports Producer as well as a massive Leicester City supporter.

As a 10-year-old schoolboy, Geoff would play in goal and write match reports. Not only that, but he'd bravely read them out in front of everyone in assembly! There would be only one career for him.

After a spell on the now-defunct Leicester Trader, and working for his future co-commentator Neville Foulger at Leicester News Service, Geoff joined BBC Radio Leicester as a sports reporter. Two years down the line, and having just celebrated his 21st birthday, he became the station's Head of Sport, a position he held for a further two years.

From there he took a career break, working abroad in places such as Ibiza and Egypt, and became a successful nightclub DJ and promoter, a passion which stretched back to his early teenage years.

Geoff, who's single, still lives in Leicestershire and watches City as often as possible when he's in the country.

AUTHOR FACTFILE

Name: Geoff Peters.
Born: 2nd April 1973; Kirby Muxloe, Leicestershire.
Supports: Leicester City. For various reasons he also likes Liverpool and Southampton.
Educated: Danemill Primary, Enderby; Brockington High, Enderby; Lutterworth Grammar.
Ambition at school: To be a sports journalist.
Career high: Becoming the BBC's youngest ever Sports Producer at 21.
First City match: Home to Manchester United, February 1981. City won 1-0.
Most memorable match: City 2 Derby 1, Wembley, May 30th 1994.
Favourite player (all-time): Steve Walsh.
Favourite players (current): Muzzy Izzet, Neil Lennon.
Favourite former manager: Brian Little.
Went most beserk about a City goal: Watching the 1997 Coca-Cola Cup Final live on South African satellite TV in a hotel room overlooking the River Nile in Cairo, Egypt when Emile Heskey equalised. Pure, unadulterated joy!

AUTHOR'S DEDICATION

This book is dedicated to my family as a thank you for their support over the years. I know it hasn't been plain sailing the entire time, and I have been a bit of a handful on occasions, but they've always been there for me, which is much appreciated. Love forever.

I would also like to dedicate this book to every Leicester City supporter who, like me, shares the ups and downs of our beloved football club week in, week out. And to Martin O'Neill . . . keep up the good work!

INDIVIDUAL MESSAGES TO:

My mum Jean: How many times do I have to explain the offside rule?
My dad Henry: Thanks for taking me to Filbert Street as a kid.
My sister Diane: Have faith in your young brother.
My cousin and best mate Mark Wood: You might be stubborn, I might be cocky,
but we have a laugh, don't we?

ALSO:

John Rawling, Roger Bushby and Neville Foulger: Thanks for having faith and helping me on my way in journalism.

AND:

Glen Ames in the US of A; Phil Mansfield in the LF of E; Dan Chisholm (The Master At Work - Tenerife 95 & 98); Justin Keaney & Greg 'Forest fan' Coupe; Mark Radcliffe and Marc Riley - two of the funniest blokes in the world . . . ever! Morrissey & Marr - 'I Know It's Over'; Darren, Danni, Steve, Ross & Howie from 2wentys; Dave Royal and Cinzano Mazerati from Celebration Management; Ann Fairbrother; Any nightclub manager that pays me good money to DJ for them; 200/B4/25 (Worldwide 1989-1998); All the gorgeous KLM air stewardesses especially Annelotte; The lovely Samantha, the Bedford Rascal and fat Harry White; The Smiths, George Michael, REM and Jimmy Nail; Beavis and Butthead (very, very funny); The Shirehorses (RIP); Z Factor - Gotta Keep Pushin' (thanks Pete Tong); Mr Benson & Mr Hedges; and Margaret Thatcher, a remarkable woman, we salute you. That's it.

INTRODUCTION

LEICESTER CITY fans were beginning to despair. Not one, but two managers had departed in the space of 13 months, both in highly acrimonious circumstances. Add that to a recent relegation from the Premiership, and the picture becomes clear; all was not well at Filbert Street. So who could steady the ship and restore some pride? Step forward Martin O'Neill.

Surely nobody in late December 1995 would have predicted what was to follow during the first two years of O'Neill's reign. His transformation of the club both amazed and delighted supporters, who were tearing their hair out after recent events.

This book, compiled by a City fan FOR City fans, details O'Neill's achievements since taking over at Filbert Street. There are some great moments to relive, but it's not just promotion, the Premiership, Cup success and Europe. There were a few hairy moments here and there, and we reflect on those as well.

The rollercoaster ride of O'Neill's first two years at Leicester City is well documented here. It will, hopefully, take you through a whole range of emotions, as well as giving you an insight into the man the fans have come to worship at Filbert Street.

"Martin, Martin start the wave . . ."

PART ONE

CHAPTER ONE:

THIS CHARMING MAN

HEARD the one about the Englishman, Irishman and Scotsman? The Englishman gives up everything to be reunited with his first true love. The Scotsman gives up everything as well, but he does it for the love of something quite different. And the (Northern) Irishman gives up on nothing and becomes a folk hero. Doesn't really make sense does it? But that's football for you.

Even the most die-hards will agree that Leicester City fans can be a fickle bunch when it comes to praising and criticising players and managers, but you can't fault their overall loyalty to the cause.

After the dreary years of the mid 1980s right through to the earliest part of the 90s, City supporters deserved some success. Brian Little transformed a struggling, nay poor, (old) Second Division side into a Premiership outfit even though they were ill-equipped for the top flight. The building blocks, however, were in place. Mark McGhee kept things ticking over until the lure of the Black Country lira proved too strong, and suddenly things looked bleak again.

Of course we hadn't reckoned on the arrival of Martin O'Neill to wave his magic wand and bring back the good times. But they didn't materialise straight away, of course.

If certain people had had their way, Martin O'Neill wouldn't have taken over from Mark McGhee in December 1995. Chief target for the chairman and his board was former Norwich manager Mike Walker who was out of work after getting the sack at Everton. His spell at Goodison was fraught with difficulties. But City fans knew what he could do on a shoestring budget having got Norwich into Europe, and competing with the best during a fantastic run. It was a matter of when, rather than if, Walker was coming. This seems to be the impression Walker was under as well.

The future was marked out at Filbert Street – but Mark McGhee wasn't in it.

DECEMBER 11th 1995
Ten days before O'Neill eventually took charge, bookmakers had installed Mike Walker as the 2-1 favourite with Alan Buckley, Dave Bassett, Trevor Francis, Steve Walsh, Danny Wilson, Howard Kendall and Ron Atkinson also in the running. Even though O'Neill was the first choice a year previous before deciding to stay at Wycombe, his name was apparently not in the frame.

DECEMBER 12th
What a difference a day makes as 24 hours later, the *Leicester Mercury* splashed with the back page headline O'NEILL JOINS RUNNING even though columnist Bill Anderson wasn't sure he'd get the job. He wrote:

"For O'Neill to be a genuine contender, he would somehow have to make an apology for wasting City's time a year ago. Then he went all the way down the line, even to the extent of having signing talks, before electing to stay at Wycombe. The humiliation it caused City is still fresh enough in the memory for him to be looked at in a rather jaundiced manner."

DECEMBER 13th
No surprise as the news came through that Mark McGhee had been appointed as the new manager of Wolves. A compensation package between City and Wolves would eventually settle at close to a million pounds.

DECEMBER 15th/16th
Mike Walker had talks with City chairman Martin George, who also interviewed Youth Team boss David Nish, the man currently looking after first team affairs. Meanwhile, fans favourite Steve Walsh ruled himself out of contention for the time being, but who would bet against him being involved behind the scenes in the future?

Mike Walker thought the job was his . . . until O'Neill walked out on Norwich.

DECEMBER 17th

Ironically, Mike Walker was at Filbert Street the day City played his former club Norwich, working for Anglia Television. Before kick off, a buzz surrounded the ground when news filtered through that Martin O'Neill had quit as Norwich boss due to differences with the Board. In his already-written pre-match notes, O'Neill discussed why he turned down City a year ago:

"I was impressed with the Leicester set up but I had what I suppose was a nonsensical dream that Wycombe could carry on climbing the leagues."

In an amazing match, City came from two goals down to beat Norwich 3-2 thanks to a late winner from 17 year old substitute Emile Heskey.

DECEMBER 19th

Martin O'Neill was still technically a Norwich employee as chairman Robert Chase refused to accept his resignation. This meant City were unable to contact O'Neill to discuss the managerial vacancy. Chase wanted half a million pounds in compensation but eventually settled for a figure believed to be about half that.

DECEMBER 20th

Bookmakers had now refused to take bets on the City job as O'Neill was by far and away the clear favourite. Interestingly, Bill Anderson wrote in his newspaper column about O'Neill's alleged unpopularity at Carrow Road:

"On Sunday......the Norwich players looked in high spirits. To them, it was not a setback but a boost. Apparently, most of them didn't like Martin O'Neill anyway."

We can assume then that Spencer Prior and Robert Ullathorne didn't share that view, as they later became O'Neill signings at Filbert Street.

DECEMBER 21st

A cold wintry morning in the centre of Leicester and an 8.30am press conference at the club's Belvoir Drive training ground. Martin George arrived by helicopter of course while Martin O'Neill took the safer route and drove the short journey from a local hotel. O'Neill, we soon discovered, was an enthusiastic man:

"I'm not just happy about joining City, I'm ecstatic. Leicester have a tremendous amount of potential and I am determined to help them fulfil it." I asked him if he could assure fans that he wouldn't walk out like messrs Little and McGhee, and he replied: "The only way I'll be leaving is if they sack me. I have no intention of using Leicester as a stepping stone, as some might say."

O'Neill had joined City with them third in the First Division table hoping to make a swift return to the top flight. But would it be easy for the Ulsterman to get back in the Premiership at the first attempt? He said:

"I think Leicester City will be very close to promotion this year. It's easy for me to say that on my first day but I have said to the chairman I will see the two and a half years out and I hope by then we will be in the Premiership and trying to get into Europe."

Prophetic words indeed. Chairman Martin George admitted that O'Neill may have been his first choice a year ago, but this time he nearly gave the job to Mike Walker.

"I got a phone call from Robert Chase at 12.15 on Sunday to tell me what had happened. It was a shock to me," he said. "It is no secret that had the call not come, we would most likely have appointed someone else on Sunday evening. Martin is the best man for the job," George added.

Mike Walker, not surprisingly, felt let down by the club and was quick to criticise City's handling of the affair. He wasn't out of work much longer, though, and was soon back in charge at Carrow Road.

DECEMBER 22nd
O'Neill watched training for the second day running but announced that David Nish and Chris Turner would pick the team for Saturday's match at Grimsby. Elsewhere, Paul Franklin and Steve Walford left their coaching positions at Norwich, and would eventually re-join O'Neill here.

DECEMBER 23rd   DIV ONE: Grimsby 2 City 2 (Roberts, Walsh)
O'Neill's first match in the dug-out. Steve Walsh scored at both ends and the manager's main concern was a leaky defence. He joked to reporters: "If it's going to be as heart stopping as this every week, I'll be dead by Easter!"

CHRISTMAS 1995
The weather prevented O'Neill making his home bow. Matches against Ipswich and Oldham were postponed due to snow. City ended the year in third place but no-one could have predicted what was to come in the following 12 months.

Heskey: "So which of your former managers shall we go for?"

O'NEILL FACTFILE:
Born: Kilrea, Northern Ireland 1st March 1952.
Played: Forest 71-80; Norwich 80; Man City 81; Norwich 81-82; Notts Co. 83-85.
Manager: Grantham, Shepshed, Wycombe (2/90-5/95), Norwich (6/95-12/95).
Honours as a player: Captained Northern Ireland, won 64 caps;
Irish Cup 71; Division One 78; European Cup 80; League Cup 78, 79.
Honours as a manager (all at Wycombe): FA Trophy 91, 93; Bob Lord Trophy 92;
GM Vauxhall Conference 92-93; Promotion to Division Two 93-94.

THERE WAS AN ENGLISHMAN, A (NORTHERN) IRISHMAN AND A SCOTSMAN...

CHAPTER TWO:

PANIC? NO, THESE THINGS TAKE TIME

NEW YEAR'S DAY 1996   DIV ONE: Millwall 1 City 1 (Corica)

A long trip to South East London for the City camp but they came away with Martin O'Neill's unbeaten record intact. City, who remained third, should have won but too many chances went begging.

      Still, they hoped it wouldn't be long before they could call on the services of their Swedish international defender Pontus Kaamark, who'd been out through injury for three months. O'Neill said: "I have seen him in action and I know that he is a good player. In fact I have been joking that it took great players such as Frank Worthington and Keith Weller years to become legends at Filbert Street while this guy has become a hero here in only one and a half games!"

JANUARY 3rd

O'Neill watched Kaamark in the reserves at Blackpool but he lasted only a matter of seconds before coming off. O'Neill was gutted by the setback: "It's bad. He could be out for the rest of the season."

Off-target City

JANUARY 6th   FA CUP ROUND 3: City 0 Manchester City 0

O'Neill eventually faced the home crowd but a dull goalless draw against a far from impressive Manchester City side failed to excite the fans.

JANUARY 13th   DIV ONE: Stoke City 1 City 0

As Wolves announced their intention to make bids for the Australian duo of Steve Corica and Zeljko Kalac, City went to Stoke where O'Neill tasted defeat for the first time. It was the injury situation causing O'Neill most headaches: "We have some problems," he admitted. Another trip to Stoke later in the season would reap huge rewards.

JANUARY 17th   FA CUP ROUND 3 REPLAY: Manchester City 5 City 0

On the face of it, O'Neill probably fancied his chances in the FA Cup replay at Manchester City. Alan Ball's side were struggling in the Premiership having scored just 12 goals in 22 outings. But things went horribly wrong as the team were humiliated. And it could have been double the score. O'Neill was shell-shocked: "We were well beaten. The team has been conceding a lot of goals this season and it would be nice to think there is an easy solution. But there isn't so we will have to address that very quickly. It is a learning process regarding the players I have got."

Not yet a month into the job and already O'Neill was having to deal with a few fans moaning about results and the team's performances.

JANUARY 21st   DIV ONE: City 0 Sunderland 0

Another televised fixture for City, and even though they failed to score in front of the home supporters, this was no disgrace against their promotion rivals.

However, player unrest soon materialised as Steve Corica questioned his future under O'Neill. The Australian midfielder said: "I want to know what's going on. Mark McGhee was the man who brought me to this country and I have great respect for the guy."

LATE JANUARY

Speculation about Corica and Wolves continued; O'Neill was linked with a swap deal involving Norwich's Andy Johnson and City's Mark Robins; And defender Steve Walsh talked about the forthcoming months: "Promotion is still there for the taking. We need to act quickly and the next month is going to be vital."

FEBRUARY 3rd   DIV ONE: City 1 (Roberts) Luton 1

Another poor display culminated in a dull home draw with Luton. Fans singled out Lee Philpott on this occasion . . . he was booed when he came ON the pitch as sub. City slipped to seventh place. Despite the supporters' frustrations, Martin O'Neill said he wasn't afraid to make big decisions about any of the players: "I am going to make changes and there could be moves which some people will view as unpopular, even bizarre, but I am sure I will get things right."

Once again, the City board came in for criticism from supporters and Martin George sympathised: "To be honest I see their point and share their frustration. I haven't seen the team win since the Norwich match either."

FEBRUARY 10th   DIV ONE: Portsmouth 2 City 1 (Roberts)

An injury time goal consigned City to defeat at Portsmouth and put them back to 10th in the table, their lowest position of the season. Ironically, this was a game they should have won but luck was not on O'Neill's side as he suffered his worst run as manager.

He said defiantly: "I will win. I've been doing it for six years as a manager and I have no doubt I will do so again. I am sure the win we need to turn the corner is not far away."

George: "The fans are great here. They'll never abuse you." O'Neill: "That's a relief."

FEBRUARY 13th
O'Neill was no doubt interested to read in the morning papers that Birmingham's much travelled striker Steve Claridge had threatened to leave St Andrews if he didn't get a pay rise. He said: "There's no reason why I shouldn't cash in on my present form before it's too late." One of O'Neill's transfer targets, Neil Lennon from Crewe, was involved in talks with Ron Atkinson, and the Northern Ireland midfielder was set to sign for Coventry before the end of the week.

FEBRUARY 15th
A busy day of transfer activity and speculation. O'Neill controversially agreed to sell Steve Corica and Zeljko Kalac to Mark McGhee at Wolves for a joint fee of £1.7 million. Another former City boss Brian Little was in touch with O'Neill as he expressed an interest to sign Julian Joachim for £1.2 million. These deals would enable O'Neill to finance his own signings as he was officially linked with Steve Claridge. And Neil Lennon announced that he wouldn't be moving to Coventry, keeping the door open for O'Neill to pounce.

FEBRUARY 17th   DIV ONE: City 1 (Taylor) Port Vale 1
City's home draw with Vale was overshadowed by a fans' demonstration against the sale of Corica. Windows were broken in the Carling Stand by a few hardcore troublemakers. O'Neill tried to calm the flames of fury by revealing that the young Aussie wasn't happy at Filbert Street. "Steve asked me if he could go four times. His agent said he was adamant that he wanted to go to Wolves. Under these circumstances there was not much anyone could have done about it," O'Neill revealed.

FEBRUARY 20th
On the eve of City's so-called grudge match with Wolves, O'Neill announced that Mark McGhee had made a bid for striker Iwan Roberts. Conscious of the fact that City are seen as a selling club, O'Neill issued a hands-off warning: "I've got no interest in selling Roberts. I want him to stay here at the club, continue to score goals and help us win a place in the Premiership."

FEBRUARY 21st   DIV ONE: Wolves 2 City 3 (Roberts, Heskey 2)

Exactly two months to the day from when he took over, and still searching for a victory, Martin O'Neill had no problems rallying the players for the trip to Molyneux. Emile Heskey scored twice as City came from behind to take all three points in a thriller.

Believe in yourselves

O'Neill tells
City to have
confidence

O'Neill's first win, at the tenth attempt, was a new club record. The late Jock Wallace had the previous worst, managing his first victory in his eighth match as boss. Regardless of that, O'Neill couldn't conceal his delight in the post match press interviews: "We played very well with quite a bit of passion. To come from behind was very satisfying. We were definitely up for it against a Wolves side who are very good."

Mark McGhee was gracious in defeat by his old club saying he didn't begrudge City the three points: "The good players I know they've got played very well and the manager maybe needs the points more than me. It's a bad result for us but it's not the end of the world."

Earlier in the day, *Leicester Mercury* football writer Graham Melton, a man considered to be more in tune with the fans than the paper's main correspondent, offered these thoughts on O'Neill, and his effect on the supporters:

"After nine games - not seasons, months, or even weeks - there are more than just rumblings of discontent. O'Neill's failure, if you call it that, is a simple one . . . his team have not won in nine games. They have avoided defeat in six, but for the average supporters these days, that is not enough. Like most managers, he has his own ideas about tactics and players, but again it takes time."

Meanwhile, Birmingham boss Barry Fry called off the Steve Claridge deal. For the time being at least.

FEBRUARY 23rd

Julian Joachim, a product of the Filbert Street youth set up, was sold to Aston Villa for a fee of £1.5 million. O'Neill revealed: "Brian Little asked me yesterday if we could do something with Julian. I spoke to the chairman and we agreed a price. What I'm doing is generating some money so I can get one or two players in. We looked at the situation and with Heskey making such rapid progress, we felt we could do something."

Had the sale come a year or 18 months earlier, there would no doubt have been a big uproar from the supporters. But because the youngster had failed to live up to his early promise, most fans felt it was 'a good bit of business'. Half the money City received went out the same day as Neil Lennon signed from Crewe. The Northern Ireland international joined City for £750,000. And the Steve Claridge deal was now 'on' again.

Two-goal Emile Heskey kills off Mark McGhee's Wolves.

FEBRUARY 24th   DIV ONE: Reading 1 City 1 (Lewis)

Neil Lennon was both hero and villain on his debut at Reading. After setting up the opening goal for Neil Lewis, he conceded a harsh penalty and the match ended in stalemate. O'Neill said: "The match obviously hinged on that penalty . . . it was a hard decision. I know it sounds like whingeing but it isn't." Lennon added: "I wanted the ground to swallow me up."

The result left City in sixth place and after the match, Steve Claridge's name cropped up again. The deal was now 'off' after he failed to agree personal terms.

FEBRUARY 28th   DIV ONE: City 0 Derby 0

First Division leaders Derby, 14 points clear of City AND with a game in hand, came to Filbert Street and couldn't gain revenge for City's win earlier in the campaign. O'Neill wasn't too unhappy: "We have to start winning at home. The plus points were that we did not concede a goal, and we put up a strong performance."

MARCH 1st

The on-off transfer saga involving Birmingham's Steve Claridge was finally resolved when he became City's second most expensive signing at £1.2 million. He said: "I was just desperate to leave. Before the move was the worst period of my life." O'Neill too was delighted the deal had been done and dusted: "Steve is a good strong attacker and I am pleased he has at last become a Leicester City player. I'm sure he can do a good job for us and help the challenge for promotion." How true that turned out to be.

MARCH 3rd   **DIV ONE: Ipswich 4 City 2 (Roberts 2)**
Claridge made his debut at Portman Road on a miserable, wet, grey Sunday afternoon. City were three goals down inside 12 minutes but managed to make a fight of it. Claridge failed to score but his future striker partner Ian Marshall got two for Ipswich. Martin O'Neill targetted the defence as cause of major concern: "We have really got to look at the situation now. This was a big game for us and we took liberties. We are not good enough to take liberties." City slipped back to 10th

Chairman Martin George made a typically vain attempt to appease supporters by revealing he'd make cash available to the manager. "It is not necessarily the case that we will only spend what we have raised in sales. If we need to do more than that, then we will."

MARCH 4th
A clearly unhappy O'Neill cancelled the players' day off and dragged them into the training ground. He made them watch a 'video nasty' .....a re-run of Sunday's horror show at Ipswich. "We never even got off the bus at Portman Road," were his incisive comments. He also threatened Claridge that if he didn't smarten up and start wearing shin pads, "I'll fine him heavily."

MARCH 9th   **DIV ONE: City 2 (Heskey 2) Grimsby 1**
At last! A home win for O'Neill to enjoy. The victory came courtesy of two Heskey goals, the latter causing some controversy. "The breaks have gone against us recently," said O'Neill, "and if Emile did handle or throw the ball in for the winner, I don't give a damn. We deserved to win and that's all there is to it."

Claridge, making his home debut, was named man of the match but paid tribute to Heskey: "I'd like to check his birth certificate to prove he's only 18!"

Meanwhile, City sold Richard Smith to Grimsby for £50,000.

MARCH 13th   **DIVE ONE: City 0 Ipswich 2**
Just 10 days after meeting at Portman Road, City entertained Ipswich in a re-arranged fixture at Filbert Street. Once again they were beaten and once again Ian Marshall got on the scoresheet. O'Neill remained positive: "All is not lost. It may sound like a forlorn hope, but we can still pick up positive points from the game -- and I still think we can win promotion." City slid back to eighth.

MARCH 15th
The club reluctantly revealed that Garry Parker had been stripped of the captaincy, axed from the squad and would probably not play for City again after 'an incident'.

MARCH 16th   **DIV ONE: Oldham 3 City 1 (Whitlow)**
Steve Walsh took over the skipper's armband for the trip to Boundary Park where City lost a dire match, and had Neil Lennon sent off. O'Neill was furious: "If teams earned goals against us I wouldn't mind but we just can't defend at crucial moments. If this goes on, then we can forget about promotion. People have now got to stand up and be counted for their places. The way we are defending at the moment, I could get someone from a convent to do a better job!"

MARCH 19th

Garry Parker was officially put on the transfer list. "I've told him he can leave," said O'Neill. "It's better for all concerned that he finds another club." Other results combined to see City slide back to 10th.

O'Neill was also angry because Mark McGhee had now decided he didn't want Zeljko Kalac at Molyneux due to work permit complications. Kalac came back to Filbert Street and without touching a ball again, he still had a role to play in City's rollercoaster season.

MARCH 23rd   DIV ONE: City 2 (Carey, Taylor) Millwall 1

They say a week is a long time in politics, and it's the same in football. It was also long enough for Parker and O'Neill to patch up their differences. The former Forest and Villa midfielder set up both goals and City climbed to eighth.

So the O'Neill/Parker affair was consigned to history but what actually happened on the night in question is still not totally clear as different players give different accounts of the story. I understand that the incident occurred during the half time interval of the match with Ipswich when Parker was unhappy with comments O'Neill was making to young full back Neil Lewis. Parker stood up for Lewis and a cup containing tea, orange juice or water went flying, staining O'Neill's suit.

In an interview with the highly respected *Fox* fanzine, O'Neill was asked about the dressing room shenanigans. "To me, what happens in the dressing room is our business," he said. "I'm not the sort of manager who believes in cameras in there and that sort of thing. What happened, believe it or not, was blown out of all proportion and certainly didn't leave those four walls via myself."

MARCH 28th

Transfer deadline day. Central defender Julian Watts joined City from Sheffield Wednesday for a fee of £210,000. Another arrival was the largely unknown Mustafa 'Muzzy' Izzet, on loan from Chelsea. Both had important roles in the push for promotion.

O'Neill's agony

MARCH 30th   DIV ONE: City 0 Sheffield United 2

One of the most significant dates in Martin O'Neill's Filbert Street diary. A watershed in many ways. A day that brought matters to a head and probably had O'Neill thinking he'd made a mistake in joining City. The football was appalling and the result even worse. The fans staged a massive demonstration, bigger than many had seen for a long time, as things hit boiling point outside the ground. Chants of "O'Neill out" and "F**k off O'Neill" were widely heard.

Afterwards, a cross section of supporters met with board members Tom Smeaton and John Elsom, as well as O'Neill. The club said: "The meeting lasted for about an hour and that was just a chance for the supporters to air their views and frustrations." O'Neill, clearly stung by the criticism, had to face the press to give his side of things.

He said: "This is the first time it has been directed at me personally. You just have to battle through these things. I am not the first manager to take stick from people and I'm sure I will not be the last. I am determined to get it right." Of the match itself, O'Neill was none too impressed: "We played very poor, the poorest we have played since I came here."

Pressure group Blue Tuesday were impressed by O'Neill's willingness to talk to fans: "It showed he has a lot of bottle and he said this was the nadir of his career. He gave us some straight answers and we, the fans, appreciated that."

Cliff Ginetta, from the official supporters club, told the *Mercury*: "The protesters had a point. The display was inept and disgraceful. People aren't going to take it much longer." But he did urge supporters to get behind the team and the manager and help them to promotion.

After all this, City were still in ninth place. The race for promotion would prove to be a thrilling one.

Worried looks all round against Sheffield United. A Nightmare on Filbert Street.

CHAPTER THREE:

YOU JUST HAVEN'T EARNED IT YET

THERE was hardly any time for the dust to settle from the weekends events when City made back to back visits to the capital. It was never going to be easy but they came through though with all guns blazing.

APRIL 2nd   DIV ONE: Charlton 0 City 1 (Claridge)
Steve Claridge brought a smile back to O'Neill's face with a wonder strike. This was despite him being on medication. He claimed: "I had a massive problem. At one stage I had all the symptoms of MS and it was very, very worrying." The goal was his first in a City shirt and first in any shirt for a long while. He added: "This one was on colour TV. It feels like the last time I scored it was on black and white!"

       O'Neill also took time to reflect on the previous weekends trauma at Filbert Street. Clearly he was wound up inside: "I thought that, with only 13 weeks into the job, I might have had more time. I accept that the fans have paid their money and have the right to moan and groan but I was really disappointed by what happened."

APRIL 6th   DIV ONE: Crystal Palace 0 City 1 (Roberts)
A swift return to the capital for City and another welcome three away points. O'Neill said: "There's certainly been a togetherness in the last two games." After missing the Sheffield United debacle due to other business, chairman Martin George rallied to O'Neill's defence by saying: "I well remember that when Brian Little got spat upon, when it was expected we would be in the top two but weren't, you know, it all turned around after that."

APRIL 9th   DIV ONE: City 1 (Robins) West Bromwich Albion 2
Buoyed by those fantastic victories, City welcomed West Brom hoping to press ahead in the race for the play offs. However, a sickening injury time goal sent City crashing to defeat. To cap that, top scorer Iwan Roberts was ruled out for the rest of the season with rib damage, a similar injury to the one which nearly prevented him going to Wembley in 1994. "Maybe it's a good omen," said the Welsh striker, "we might win there again."

APRIL 13th   DIV ONE: Tranmere 1 City 1 (Robins)
Struggling Tranmere put another dent in City's promotion ambitions at Prenton Park.
Neil Lennon's unlucky deflected own goal meant City had to settle for a point. They
stood in eighth place, three points off the play off zone. O'Neill remained positive:
"The supporters who came saw some terrific football from us, but it's not about
terrific football now. It's about results."

     Meanwhile, O'Neill prepared to contact his counterpart at Chelsea, Glenn
Hoddle, to get Muzzy Izzet's loan spell extended. "He's a very good player who has
done well for us."

APRIL 17th   DIV ONE: City 2 (Claridge 2) Oldham 0
Steve Claridge began a good run of form by grabbing both goals in front of just
12,790 fans at Filbert Street. Claridge though was oozing confidence: "The way
we're playing, we've no-one to fear in this league." Claridge's strike partner Emile
Heskey received a massive boost when he was called into the England Under 18
squad for the forthcoming European Youth Finals in France.

APRIL 20th   DIV ONE: City 2 (Walsh, Claridge) Huddersfield 1
On-song Claridge grabbed the match winner to keep City in the hunt and the striker
said: "At least we've given ourselves a chance. After the Sheffield United game,
you'd have said that that was a touch improbable." O'Neill, though, wouldn't get
carried away. "It's still not totally in our hands as Ipswich have a game in hand but
I'm thrilled to bits by this." Meanwhile, Chelsea agreed to extended Muzzy Izzet's
loan spell until the end of the season.

Million-pound striker Steve Claridge: He scored five in seven in April 1996.

APRIL 27th   DIV ONE: City 3 (Claridge, Heskey, Lennon) Birmingham 0
Birmingham had lost their way in the league after being promotion contenders earlier in the season, perhaps due to an extended Coca-Cola Cup run, and they didn't pose City too many problems in this game. Claridge, against his former club, was delighted to score to make it five in seven. City ended the day in sixth, but below them, Ipswich had a game in hand.

MAY 1st
That game in hand was against Huddersfield, another team with ever decreasing play off aspirations. Ipswich's 2-1 victory lifted them to sixth and left City seventh on goals scored with just one match to play. It was now completely out of City's hands.

May 5th   DIV ONE: Watford 0 City 1 (Izzet)

Defeat at Graham Taylor's Watford would have ended Leicester's play off hopes, a draw would only be good enough if Ipswich were beaten so they had to go for a win and then hope others failed. Muzzy Izzet's header on the hour earned City the points and consigned the Hornets to relegation. City finished in fifth, and set up a two-leg showdown with fourth placed Stoke.

Izzet the goalscorer was buzzing after this one: "I can't believe it, I'm so delighted. I want to stay here . . . I definitely want to become a Leicester City player full time."

Skipper Steve Walsh, a veteran of the play-offs, felt victory was hard earned. He said: "I think we deserved to win at Watford and deserve to be in the play-offs. It didn't look good six weeks ago but we've managed to grind out results which is a good sign."

A tense time for O'Neill in the race for the play-offs.

CHAPTER FOUR:

ROAD TO WEMBLEY (PART ONE)

THE First Division play-offs have been dominated by Leicester City in recent years but could they pull it off again, like they did when big Walshie destroyed Derby in 1994? I suppose after the season they'd just had, anything was possible.

MAY 12th   DIVISION ONE PLAY-OFF SEMI-FINAL 1ST LEG:
                                      City 0 Stoke 0

Lou Macari's Stoke, who did the double over City during the season, were confident visitors to Filbert Street for the first leg. A nerve wracking afternoon produced no goals but plenty of drama, and come full time it was City who were the happier, having kept a clean sheet. That was thanks in the main to goalkeeper Kevin Poole. Signed by Brian Little in the summer of 1991, Poole had seen off several pretenders to his crown, and despite his apparent lack of height, had made some terrific saves over the years. Admittedly, there had been one or two howlers but then most keepers are guilty of them from time to time.

It was Poole's afternoon in many ways. One save at the far post was miraculous to say the least, clawing the ball out when it seemed he was beaten. O'Neill was full of praise for him: "He made two fantastic saves, and the second one from a point blank header at the far post . . . well, I just don't know how he kept that one out. We are still in the hunt and will go to Stoke knowing that we have a good chance

MAY 15th   DIVISION ONE PLAY-OFF SEMI-FINAL 2ND LEG:
                                    Stoke 0 City 1 (Parker)

The last time City needed to travel for the second leg was 1993 when they took a 1-0 lead to Portsmouth, and drew 2-2 on the night. That scoreline (after extra time) would have been enough to see City through at Stoke, on the away goals rule. The tension was unbearable at the Victoria Ground, even though the play-offs were nothing new for City fans.

After a goalless first half, City came out with more purpose and while some were still taking their seats, the main drama unfolded. Heskey battled his way to the byline and scrambled a cross to the far post. Who was there to meet it? None other than Garry Parker, who just two months before was on his way out of Filbert Street after that infamous bust up with Martin O'Neill. His volley from a tight angle sparked off jubilation behind the goal where several thousand City fans were seated. Could this be the moment that takes us to Wembley, they thought. Three quarters of an hour later and it was all over. Even Stoke fans who invaded the pitch couldn't dampen City's delight.

Parker's winning goal (not his final strike of the season, of course) did seem quite unlikely back in March as the player himself admitted: "I was knocking on the gaffer's door all the time wanting to get back into the side but the lads just kept on winning and I just had to accept that."

O'Neill, who deserves credit for bringing Parker back for such a high profile occasion, admitted: "We were excellent under difficult circumstances. I am delighted, but the result was the most important thing. I said to the lads at half time that there was no point in playing well if you don't go on to win the game."

Supporters club chief Cliff Ginetta, no doubt speaking on behalf of the fans, said: "When Mark McGhee left as manager, he said he wanted to manage a big club. Martin O'Neill is now poised to turn us into that big club."

Wembley here we come! (Not for me though . . . Ibiza needed uncovering!!!)

The naked truth: Post-match euphoria at Stoke.

MAY 16th-MAY 26th

Back to business, and the usual scramble for match tickets ensued. There was also the scramble for unusual pre-Wembley stories; Steve Claridge's gambling habits guaranteed him plenty of back page coverage in the build-up: "I won there with Cambridge in the play offs, and with Birmingham in the Auto Windscreen Shield last season. Palace are strong but we can beat them." I wonder if he bet on himself to get the winner?

Meanwhile, the only City captain to lift a trophy at Wembley, Simon Grayson, was looking forward to seeing his big pal Steve Walsh do the same: "The confidence here is very high and I see no reason why Walshie shouldn't climb the steps to hold the trophy like I did."

For Martin O'Neill, Wembley was a familiar stage having been there during his time with Wycombe. Did he ever believe they could get to this stage? "Going to Wembley - and the chance of getting into the Premiership - is something I have never lost sight of, even though we had so much to do. After drawing at Tranmere, I remember saying to the players that we needed 10 points out of the 12 available to get to the play offs. But when we arrived back at Filbert Street, and I was getting off the bus, I told them, 'Better make that 12' and so it proved."

Claridge shows perfect timing

MAY 27th   DIV ONE PLAY-OFF FINAL @ Wembley:
                        Palace 1 City 2 (Parker, Claridge) AET

After much agonising on team selection, O'Neill stuck with the same starting eleven which had won at Stoke in the second leg. But soon after kick off things went wrong as Palace took the lead through Andy Roberts. That (unlucky-for-City) 13th minute goal stood until (unlucky-for-Palace) 13 minutes from the end, when Muzzy Izzet was chopped down in the penalty area. Cool as you like, Garry Parker slotted home the resulting spot kick to set up a grandstand finish. Parker later admitted: "It's amazing. It's only the second penalty we've had all season. I do think we were the better side even though we needed a bit of luck."

Try as they might, neither side could break the deadlock inside normal time so extra time arrived. Let's bear in mind at this point that despite their frequent trips to Wembley, they hadn't needed extra time before. Would it take its toll on the players?

As the seconds ticked away at the end of the extra 30 minutes, no-one could reasonably have guessed what was to happen next. A stoppage in play allowed O'Neill to bring on calamity keeper Zeljko Kalac for Kevin Poole because his height (6'7" apparently) could help in a penalty shoot out. Kalac revealed: "I knew what the plan was, but I wasn't really needed." Poole added: "It would have been an injustice for us to have lost, especially if it had been on penalties."

Penalty king Garry Parker ignites City's spark at Wembley.

This inspired substitution paid off for O'Neill, although not quite in the manner he expected. The arrival of the giant 'Spider' seemed to distract the Palace players (as well as both sets of fans!) as a free kick floated towards the goal. The ball dropped to Claridge on the edge of the box, and, according to most observers, time stood still. Time in which Super Stevie, with socks around his ankles, managed to hack the ball goalwards, past a flat footed Nigel Martyn, and into the net. GOAL. Surely the winner. Claridge set off towards the City fans, who, in the 1994 words of Alan Parry, were in 'dreamland'.

The re-start was pretty much academic as the final whistle went straight after and Martin O'Neill could celebrate a truly remarkable few months at Filbert Street. "I think we played brilliantly. Even when we went a goal behind we never lost heart. Claridge my star man? Close, but Neil Lennon was the best player on the pitch, he was world class. But we had plenty of heroes out there. It was certainly a long way from the Sheffield United game which was a bit of a debacle, but such is football. Oh, it's just fantastic."

For Steve Claridge, the bookies' friend, it was fantasy time: "That was the biggest moment of my career. Was it a mis-hit? To be honest I can't remember. It sat up and I might have shinned it. But does it really matter?" Er, no. Not at all.

Skipper Steve Walsh beamed widely from side to side as he led his troops up the famous steps. A reward for his years of loyalty, but would he carry on playing next season? Painkillers were helping him through continuous injuries and the player wasn't sure whether this was truly it: "I definitely want to continue. I'm going to think it over during the summer."

The next day, Walsh led the squad on a victorious open top bus journey through Leicester to mark their achievement and for O'Neill, it was nice to see the supporters on his side: "What a fantastic reception from the fans. The players deserve it. I certainly don't want to see City relegated next season. People will say we've only got the one season up there, but I think we'll stay up."

So could City's loyal army of fans expect to see the board bankroll some big signings? No of course not. This is Leicester City we're talking about. Chairman Martin George's initial reaction was not to dip his hand into his own pocket (which to be fair he didn't have to), but to try and get others to cough up. He told the *Mercury*: "We would welcome financial support from any source. There is a perception that we are a closed shop. That has never been the case and the door is open for anyone to come in and back us." There were not many takers, you may not be surprised to read.

When time stood still at Wembley. Claridge: "Oh damn, I've gone and shinned it . . ."

*Who needs
Cantona, when
we've got Mustafa?*

Days later, City revealed that season ticket prices were to increase for the Premiership campaign. Supporters were not happy, as you'd expect. The average increase was 18 per cent. Martin George said: "We believe that the season tickets represent excellent value for money."

Many fans were off on holiday, proudly wearing the new kit around the world, looking forward to the big time again. Season 96-97 surely couldn't be more dramatic?

Premier League, here we come!

CHAPTER FIVE:

MONEY CHANGES EVERYTHING

SUMMER 1996

Despite the euphoria of the Wembley win and subsequent promotion to the Premiership, the summer months, June and July in particular, were not the happiest time for Martin O'Neill. The main problem was a status report on the club which they themselves commissioned. This report highlighted division in the boardroom over the appointment of O'Neill. It appears that chairman Martin George stuck his neck out to land O'Neill, even though other directors wanted Mike Walker to take over the void left by Mark McGhee.

The report also said a number of directors questioned O'Neill's experience in the transfer market when it came to big signings, and even the team's style of play. Not only that, but it indicated that had City not made it to the Premiership, O'Neill would have been sacked to make way for Walker. O'Neill was on holiday when the report came to light, and was said to be 'angry and furious' - especially as it had come AFTER the Wembley success.

O'Neill hits back

Speaking in the *Leicester Mercury*, O'Neill raged: "I found the report staggeringly off the mark. If the managers role is in accordance with the report, he might as well not bother turning up. Like it or not, at a football club, he is the most important man; yet the report, if implemented, would make his influence negligible. As for certain directors not backing me, I could understand around the Christmas time why board members were reluctant to take me on, perhaps seeing me in the same light as Mark McGhee because I had walked out on Norwich.

"I suppose when results went poorly, certain rumblings were inevitable. But I have to say I turned it round so much in a short space of time. I thought the fans who demonstrated against me had not given me enough time, only 13 weeks, and the same went for certain members of the board," he added.

The City boss may also have felt his job was far from secure when Martin George, his chief champion amongst the directors, was voted out as chairman. But before handing over to Tom Smeaton, who was vice chairman, George, unhappy at losing his position, tried to force his successor's financial dealings by revealing: "I am delighted to stand down on the basis that a total of £6 million for players and plans for £5 million to be spent on the popular side will be in the offing." And in a dig at those in the boardroom who didn't back O'Neill 100%, he added: "I am sure you will be told that everyone now supports the manager. That would be said wouldn't it." George remained on the board and Smeaton gave the manager his full backing.

Not everyone thought the seat-swapping by directors was the best thing for the club. Cliff Ginetta, from the supporters club, argued: "It's just the same old singers and the same old song. I can't see the point of making changes for changes sake."

Former England striker and now TV pundit Jimmy Greaves felt the board would have to make enormous amounts of money available if City were to stand a prayer back in the top flight. He said: "They have to spend £20 million to keep City up. I can't see how they're going to hold their position with the team they've got."

The summer was also full of speculation about who would be coming to Filbert Street for the new campaign, as well as stories linking current players to other clubs. The squad needed strengthening as Martin O'Neill was only too aware: "We have the nucleus of a good side and there is also a great camaraderie, but we don't have enough strength in depth for the top flight."

In the space of a few days, O'Neill revealed his interest in Millwall full back Ben Thatcher. A fee of £1.8 million was agreed, the player too agreed personal terms and went away to think about it. O'Neill got wind that Thatcher was also talking to Wimbledon and he pulled the plug. Angry at this, O'Neill fumed: "Leicester are too big a club to be trifled with."

On-loan midfielder Muzzy Izzet got his wish of a permanent deal as City paid Chelsea £650,000 for his services. But on his way out, among others, was striker Iwan Roberts. He joined Wolves for over £1 million after pay negotiations broke down between O'Neill and Roberts' agent, the former City player David Speedie.

O'Neill was linked with several high-profile players, most notably Wimbledon hitman Dean Holdsworth, Norwich wonderkid Darren Eadie, and Swedish international Jesper Blomqvist. These, however, came to nothing.

The search goes on!

I won't sign men
for the sake of
it, says O'Neill

His first 'new' signings, if you discount that of Izzet, came just 48 hours before the start of the season. By now fans had become impatient. Instead of trusting his judgement in the transfer market (Lennon, Claridge, Watts and Izzet all a success), panic set in. Despite this, season ticket sales were very good. Proof if proof be needed that City fans are extremely loyal. Most of them at most of the time anyway!!

Two months after the Sheffield United game, O'Neill's popularity increases a bit . . .

The arrivals on the eve of the campaign had both come from lower divisions. O'Neill had returned to his former club Norwich to sign solid central defender Spencer Prior for £600,000. And he splashed out just under a million on Millwall's American international goalkeeper Kasey Keller. Prior was clearly relishing the challenge ahead, and spoke highly of O'Neill: "The manager is a great motivator and I am sure we will be good enough to stay up. It's a big challenge because everyone is writing us off. That makes me more determined to prove everyone wrong."

The spending would not stop there, promised new chairman Tom Smeaton: "Despite today's signings, there are substantial funds for the manager to spend. But that should not put extra pressure on him. He will use it when he's ready."

So the team which would start the season would not look too dissimilar to the one that finished at the end of May. O'Neill clearly intended to carry on spending, but only sign players when the timing was absolutely right. His transfer market activity, although limited, had been, and would continue to be, impeccable through out the coming months.

CHAPTER SIX:

THERE IS A LIGHT THAT NEVER GOES OUT

ON PAPER, it was not the toughest start to the season imaginable - newly promoted Sunderland and perennial strugglers Southampton as the opening two fixtures. But, as any cliche-ridden footballer will tell you, there are no easy games in the Premiership.

AUGUST 17th   PREM: Sunderland 0 City 0
New recruits Kasey Keller and Spencer Prior not surprisingly made their debuts at Sunderland's Roker Park in a repeat of the opening fixture in the First Division 12 months previous. City won 2-1 on that occasion but had to settle for a share of the spoils this time. Both debutants worked hard and came out of the game with credit. Martin O'Neill was happy but announced he was still on the lookout: "I would still like more new faces and money is still available."

AUGUST 21st   PREM: City 2 (Heskey 2) Southampton 1
The last time City were in the Premiership, they had to wait until mid-September to get their first win. Not so long this time, thankfully, as young starlet Emile Heskey scored both goals, one of which was an absolute beauty and enough to impress watching England manager Glenn Hoddle. Heskey, only 18, earned an England Under 21 call up after this display. Despite Heskey's two-goal super show, it was an all round effort to get the three points, according to the City boss: "The lads played great in the first half and deserved to be ahead. We lost our way a bit later but they did magnificently to hold on. It was a fine result for us." O'Neill also revealed that John Robertson, a former Nottingham Forest team-mate, was his new assistant manager.

AUGUST 24th   PREM: City 0 Arsenal 2
The unbeaten run of two games, which had elevated City to seventh in the early published league tables, was always going to be under threat as soon as Arsenal came to town. City may have been beaten, but they emerged with credit and their heads held high. O'Neill said: "Four points from three games is not so bad, and we will take it from there."

Midfield ace Scott Taylor believed City weren't out of their depth as many pundits predicted: "I thought that we more than matched them and deserved to get something out of the game. It does prove that we can compete at the highest level, but we feel we were unlucky."

AUGUST 30th

O'Neill, not unhappy with the start to the season, was already on the look out for new players armed with some of Tom Smeaton's promised cash. The chequebook came out again after just three matches when he signed Ipswich striker Ian Marshall for just under a million pounds. Although Marshall is not the youngest and fastest attacker in the country, O'Neill says his record speaks for itself: "He will give us more power and strength in attack. He is a proven goalscorer and can do very well for us at this level."

Marshall, scorer of three goals against City in the previous season, had his eye on a partnership with Steve Claridge when he said: "We are certainly going to be the most scruffiest strikeforce in the game! Seriously though, you always want to test yourself against the best. And the thought of playing against the likes of Ravanelli and Vialli is very exciting."

SEPTEMBER 2nd   PREM: Sheffield Wednesday 2 City 1 (Claridge)

Marshall had to settle for a place on the bench as City went to David Pleat's surprise table toppers. Claridge's wonderful goal was one of many positive points and O'Neill was far from downhearted. He said: "Sometimes getting hammered makes a defeat easier to accept than one by the odd goal when you know you deserved better. It is now a matter of self belief. The players may be down at the moment but they have to believe in themselves. I believe in them because they played so well."

SEPTEMBER 7th   PREM: Nottingham Forest 0 City 0

An inspired performance from goalkeeper Mark Crossley prevented City getting a rare, but deserved victory at the City Ground. In a match best remembered for Steve Stone's nasty injury, City were constantly denied by Crossley and were left very disappointed. Midfielder Neil Lennon felt it was two points dropped rather than one gained: "We were much the better side and thoroughly deserved to win. Most people thought that we would be going straight back down but the squad is getting together now and hopefully putting the critics in their place."

You sense that O'Neill was rather pleased with his team after this display....at the club where he made his name as a player: "It is very satisfying to reflect that we were in total control of a Forest side who were in Europe last season."

SEPTEMBER 10th/11th

A double dose of good news for City. Firstly, Pontus Kaamark came through a reserve team outing unscathed, almost a year after getting injured against Bolton. And a Football League tribunal ruled that Wolves would have to pay £250,000 damages to City for reneging on the Zeljko Kalac transfer. Chairman Tom Smeaton beamed: "We are delighted that the commission have found there was a breach by Wolves and that damages have been awarded."

McAteer: "Think you're hard, eh?" Heskey: "You ask Phillipe Albert . . ."

SEPTEMBER 15th   PREM: City 0 Liverpool 3
City made Liverpool sweat for the three points at Filbert Street....until half time
anyway. After the break, the Red Machine was definitely in full effect as Patrick
Berger scored twice. While accepting the quality of the opposition, O'Neill didn't
mince his words: "Our defending was poor and a lot of things need to be sorted out.
We have to get ourselves back together again."

SEPTEMBER 17th   COCA-COLA CUP (2) 1st leg:
                      Scarborough 0 City 2 (Lawrence, Izzet)

Scarborough. The Road To Wembley began here for City and the scoreline could have been more emphatic had Garry Parker not missed a penalty. Parker, whose spot kick at Wembley was as cool as you like, joked afterwards: "I can only take penalties in front of 70,000 people!"

SEPTEMBER 22nd   PREM: Tottenham 1 City 2 (Claridge, Marshall)

City's best result of the season to date came at White Hart Lane, seen live on Sky TV, as substitute Ian Marshall scored the late winner, his first for the club: "It was great to get the goal. We deserved to win the game and it showed we are not as bad as some people say." Marshall's goal spared the blushes of skipper Steve Walsh who missed a second half penalty. "I'll never take another one again. I've taken bags of stick about it," he said later. Martin O'Neill's reaction? "If we had lost this, I would have committed suicide -- just after I'd killed Walshie!"

SEPTEMBER 25th   COCA-COLA CUP (2) 2nd leg:
                      City 2 (Lawrence, Parker) Scarborough 1 (AGG 4-1)

A crowd of under 11,000 turned out to see this League Cup encounter, which City eventually won, thanks to a last minute penalty, Parker atoning for his first leg miss. Making his debut as substitute was German triallist Sascha Lenhart. He replaced Jamie Lawrence after getting knocked unconscious while scoring the opener. O'Neill was glad his players had done a professional job in what was a potential banana skin situation: "In the two games we have done enough to get there but a few Premiership sides have gone out so we are quite happy to still be in there. That said, we have not performed brilliantly."

City's reward in the third round was a trip to York, who had already dumped Everton from the competition.

SEPTEMBER 28th   PREM: City 1 (Heskey) Leeds 0

George Graham had taken over at Leeds and was making them much harder to beat. City managed to grind them down thanks to Heskey's goal....a result which left them 10th....yes, that's the top half of the table for a team tipped to be bottom! O'Neill, however, sounded his usual note of caution: "It's alright us having fantastic belief in ourselves but we needed to win a match or two to bring that through. We've now done that and are tenth in the table, but let's come back down to earth. There is still a lot to be done."

EARLY OCTOBER

International call-ups meant City had a break from League action, but it gave Martin O'Neill time to reflect on his first bite at the Premiership cherry. He said: "We have played eight games and have 11 points. We are doing okay. If you had asked me at the beginning of the season about having this situation, I would have said it wasn't too bad at all."

O'Neill's boy wonder Heskey made his England Under 21 debut in a goalless draw with Poland at Molyneux and was soon the subject of more transfer speculation, once again linking him with Liverpool, but this time for £3 million. O'Neill was having none of it and said angrily: "I wouldn't sell myself for £3 million and I can't even play!"

One player not gaining international recognition (who probably deserves it) was Muzzy Izzet who investigated the possibility of playing for Turkey. However, when he learned that to be eligible, he must serve three to four months national service, Izzet had second thoughts: "Doesn't really sound much fun does it?"

Izzet's brilliant midfield form was one of the reasons that Garry Parker wasn't getting regular first team action, so Parker went back on the transfer list. O'Neill said: "I spoke to Garry and he's unhappy. He's handed in a transfer request because he feels he should be in the team. At 31, he wants to be playing regularly and we have reluctantly agreed to let him go." Like the previous season, Parker was to fight his way back and play a big role in the second half of the campaign.

Meanwhile, O'Neill looked to strengthen his squad by taking Stuart Slater on trial. The former Celtic, West Ham and Ipswich player scored twice on his debut for the reserves.

OCTOBER 12th   PREM: City 1 (Watts) Chelsea 3
Julian Watts' first goal for City put them firmly in the driving seat against Chelsea's star studded line up but, like against Liverpool, they fell apart in the second half. City slipped to 12th and O'Neill blasted his players for a lack of concentration: "We were more than comfortable at half time. But we went to sleep at the start of the second half and allowed them back into the game. It is a great disappointment as we have been doing so well recently. You just can't switch off in this league." O'Neill was also unhappy about the referee, particularly not protecting Heskey enough. The referee was Mike Reed. The combination of Reed and Chelsea would anger him considerably more later in the season.

OCTOBER 19th   PREM: West Ham 1 City 0
While O'Neill let Mark Robins go on loan to FC Copenhagen in the Danish League, his City side succumbed to their Upton Park hoodoo. Once again they failed to win at this ground, and also had Steve Walsh sent off. Walsh and O'Neill called it 'harsh' and the manager had some choice words with referee Mike Riley at the end.

OCTOBER 22nd   COCA-COLA CUP (3): York 0 City 2 (Lennon, Grayson)
Round three of this competition was tricky for City against giantkillers York but they progressed thanks to rare goals from messrs Lennon and Grayson. O'Neill, delighted with the result but worried about a mounting casualty list, could look forward to a home tie in the fourth round with Premiership champions Manchester United.

OCTOBER 26th   PREM: City 2 (Claridge, Heskey) Newcastle 0
City continued to confound their critics with another inspired performance against so-called 'superior' opposition. This time they disposed of Kevin Keegan's flamboyant Newcastle, who a week before delighted the nation with a five-nil drubbing of Manchester United. Kasey Keller kept the ball out at one end, while Claridge and Heskey fired City's goals in a match shown live all around the world.

O'Neill clearly enjoyed speaking to the press after this match: "In a game we were expected to lose, we showed tremendous commitment all the way through. I think Newcastle are fantastic so maybe we got them on the right day, but it really is great for us."

Meanwhile, O'Neill's already limited squad was reduced further when defender Jimmy Willis was forced to retire from football due to long-standing injuries. Despite a bad start to his Filbert Street career, Willis established himself as a tough player with a never say die attitude, as O'Neill acknowledged: "We all feel sorry for Jimmy. It's a pity when this has to happen to any player and we wish him well for the future."

NOVEMBER 2nd   PREM: Derby 2 City 0
Buoyed by the Newcastle result, City came crashing back down to earth at the Baseball Ground. Injuries played their part as City dropped to 13th. O'Neill revealed: "The chairman came into the dressing room afterwards and said we must do something straight away in the transfer market." But Tom Smeaton didn't reveal how much this so-called 'substantial' figure would be. Chairmen are like that, aren't they?

O'Neill continued: "I could not have asked for more from my players. Derby were a strong, physical team as we knew they would be. But we are not quite strong enough to achieve what I want to see from us. The bottom three clubs are still somewhat adrift but that can change very quickly."

NOVEMBER 16th   PREM: Aston Villa 1 City 3 (Claridge, Parker, Izzet)
The sight of City fans actually applauding Brian Little before this game showed that forgiveness takes time. Almost two years on from his Filbert Street departure, Little had still to win against his old club, this being the third attempt. A controversial penalty, awarded by Wembley '93 "villain" David Elleray, gave City the initiative, and they capped the display with a brilliant solo Izzet goal. Of the penalty, O'Neill diplomatically said: "All that matters is that the penalty was given and we scored from it. We remember suffering a questionable penalty at Tottenham. So maybe it does even itself out."

Central defender Spencer Prior, solid as a rock in the back five, felt Villa had taken them lightly. "We showed them it was a big mistake. Now we need to do that to more teams and start a run. We also need to get out of the habit of following up a big win with a draw or defeat. If we keep doing that, then we will always be under pressure for our position in the table."

NOVEMBER 19th
For the first time since they were promoted back in May, City were no longer outright favourites for relegation. Bookmakers had them at evens, with rivals Forest, struggling at the bottom, 4-6 for the drop.

NOVEMBER 23rd   PREM: City 1 (Walsh) Everton 2

A mistake from Kevin Poole, deputising for Kasey Keller who was away on international duty, helped gift the points to Everton. O'Neill was pretty annoyed: "That was a game I thought we would win. We lost two dreadful goals. I honestly thought that we were past doing that. We just gave them two goals and you can't do that."

NOVEMBER 25th

Emile Heskey, at the centre of most City transfer speculation, decided to end all that (for the time being) by agreeing to an extension to his contract. The extra year keeps him at Filbert Street until the summer of 1999. O'Neill was very pleased the youngster had put pen to paper: "It's almost like getting a new player. It's all about ambition -- and if we have the most coveted young player signing for Leicester City for another year, then I'm delighted."

The player himself told journalists he was perfectly happy here: "You can move somewhere else and either not be happy where you are living, or be travelling up and down the motorway every day. It's good for me to be near my family."

Meanwhile, triallist Stuart Slater rejected a one-year contract in favour of a longer deal at Watford. And Mark Robins was back after his loan spell in Denmark.

NOVEMBER 27th   COCA-COLA CUP (4):
        City 2 (Claridge, Heskey) Manchester United 0

A hollow victory, some claimed, but still enormously enjoyed against a 'weakened' United side. The champions fielded lots of youngsters but did include five internationals . . . Poborsky, Keane, McClair, Cruyff and Scholes. Two days after signing that new deal, Emile Heskey stole the show, scoring one and setting up the other with an extravagant backheeled volley. O'Neill thought the win was well deserved: "I accept that in terms of Manchester United's priorities this season, this competition is not at the very top, but they came here and put out a side that still needed to be beaten. Poborsky cost more than my entire team. That gets it into perspective."

City were now 7-1 for the Cup and were drawn away at Ipswich in the quarter finals. "We would have preferred a home draw but I would have settled beforehand for just being in the hat," said O'Neill.

NOVEMBER 30th   PREM: Manchester United 3 City 1 (Lennon)

United, back to full strength, really had to battle for this victory against a City side missing Walsh, Whitlow and Taylor but giving a full league debut to youngster Stuart Campbell. It was goalless until the last 15 minutes when United stepped up a gear. O'Neill said: "I felt it was going to be our day, holding them at bay for so long with all their super players. But then they got the goal and the floodgates were wide open."

Fifteen games into the season and City were 14th with 17 points - a solid start and something to build on. Doubts, mainly in the press, still surfaced about their long term ability to stay in the Premiership, but for now the fans had something to cheer about.

Gary Lineker and Steve Walsh:
Leicester City legends
past and present.

CHAPTER SEVEN:

I KNOW IT'S GONNA HAPPEN SOMEDAY

DECEMBER 1996 marked Martin O'Neill's first anniversary at Filbert Street and as the vultures circled at struggling Nottingham Forest, supporters feared the worst. "It's Christmas . . . must be time for a new manager . . ." While they managed to hang on to their most prized asset, they only mustered 10 points from nine games in two and half months before they stuffed Derby at Filbert Street. The cup competitions, however, were providing considerable entertainment for the City faithful.

DECEMBER 3rd   PREM: Middlesbrough 0 City 2 (Claridge, Izzet)
A great start to the month for City with Muzzy Izzet scoring a tremendous second half goal to delight the travelling army of supporters who made the long Tuesday night journey to the Riverside Stadium. Izzet's midfield partner Neil Lennon enthused: "We're playing some great stuff at the moment and it's a great team to play in. We've got some big home games coming up and if we can cut out the silly mistakes there, then we've got the chance to pick up some valuable points.

The win lifted City to 12th and took them to 20 points for the season, a landmark for O'Neill to dwell on: "It's the first target for us. I still think you need 42 points before you can take any sort of breather. But we've got 20 and it's great."

DECEMBER 7th   PREM: City 1 (Marshall) Blackburn 1
The 1993/94 Premiership champions came to Filbert Street in a surprisingly low position and on a cold, foggy afternoon, the two sides scrapped it out for a draw. The bright spot on the horizon for City was the return, as substitute, of Pontus Kaamark. Ian Marshall was back in defence for City and grabbed the late equaliser. He said: "I do like scoring goals, but the most important thing is simply to be playing. I am an attacker but if I'm picked in defence, so be it."

DECEMBER 16th
Skipper Steve Walsh described his injury problems as 'a nightmare' as he faced a hernia operation: "It has taken so long for it to be diagnosed and now I'm going to be out for several weeks."

HURDY GÜRDY MÄN-MÄRKEN
SCHMØØRDËN PISHDEN BLØTTØ!

I'M ONLY ELEVEN!

DECEMBER 19th

The news City fans didn't want to hear came two days short of Martin O'Neill's first anniversary; Nottingham Forest, where O'Neill spent the best days of his playing career, had parted company with Frank Clark, one of O'Neill's former City Ground team mates. O'Neill was in the frame. It was just before Christmas. There was a sense of deja vu.

However, O'Neill soon put paid to speculation linking him with the Forest job saying: "Before anyone puts two and two together and gets five, let me say that you are going to have to put up with me for the next 18 months of my contract. I said on the day I signed that I wouldn't be walking out on the club during the contract. If I do leave before then, it will have to be done by the board or the fans. I am sure eight or nine months ago, you would have got long odds that we would be sitting around mid table in the Premiership and in the quarter finals of the Coca-Cola Cup. So, as for the other matter, I am just pleased you have put up with me so far." I guess that was as far from a resignation speech as you could get!

DECEMBER 21st   PREM: City 0 Coventry 2

No happy anniversary for O'Neill as Dion Dublin twice opened up the City defence to score against his hometown club. However, Pontus Kaamark completed his first full first team game for over a year. O'Neill: "We did not play well but the thing is that even then we had the chances to win the game, especially through Emile. We must keep reminding ourselves that he's still only 18."

Yet again, the club fed fans a story via the *Leicester Mercury* that 'some more money' was available to O'Neill. Call me a cynic - but it's funny how that only happens after the team loses . . .! O'Neill said: "God knows how much there is and God knows what I'll do with it."

DECEMBER 26th   PREM: Liverpool 1 City 1 (Claridge)

A well deserved point for City at Anfield but they led with 10 minutes left so Martin O'Neill could feel a tinge of disappointment. "I'm sure if we'd been offered a draw beforehand we would have taken it," he confessed, "but I am sitting here actually feeling disappointed we didn't win the game. But there you go. Liverpool are the only team so far this season who have really turned us over and that we come here and take a point from them is terrific."

DECEMBER 28th   PREM: City 2 (Heskey, Izzet) Nottingham Forest 2

Once again the two sides fought out a draw but Forest only snatched a point at the death as City, fielding an understrength team due to injuries, were deservedly ahead approaching full time. O'Neill said: "I thought that we were terrific considering the side we had out because of the players missing. The effort they put in was sensational." Goalscorer Izzet was less happy: "We need to start winning at Filbert Street to balance up the good away results. I can't believe we've only taken two points off them; it should be four or six."

DECEMBER 31st

At the end of 1996, City were in the relative comfort of 12th place with 23 points. Fans were also taking great satisfaction from proving the pundits wrong again and again. Oh yes . . . Forest and Derby were below City in the table!

JANUARY 1st 1997   PREM: City v Tottenham *match postponed*

Despite the lack of New Year's Day action, Martin O'Neill found himself in the thick of it off the field. Whilst driving home with his family in Buckinghamshire, he went to the aid of a man who had collapsed in the street after being kicked and punched. The national newspapers labelled him a hero. He told the *Mercury*:

"It was actually my daughter that spotted him first and I was very concerned for him because the temperature was minus four. I got my wife to call an ambulance and gave him a coat. The guy eventually recognised me and asked if he could have my autograph. I told him in his state he should be more concerned with getting to hospital. I honestly believe that I didn't do more than anyone else would have done in that situation."

JANUARY 4th   FA CUP (3): City v Southend *match postponed*

The weather continued to play havoc with the sporting programme but it gave time for injured captain Steve Walsh to reflect on the latest silverware to find its way onto his mantlepiece. Walsh, named Sports Personality of the Year by BBC East Midlands Television, said: "I am absolutely delighted with the honour which has come as a complete surprise. Some of the lads ribbed me about it when I was nominated, so to have actually won the trophy just made them even more keen to have a go at me!"

JANUARY 7th   COCA-COLA CUP QUARTER-FINAL:
                     Ipswich v City *match postponed*

Despite everyone looking forward to this Cup tie, the delay wasn't necessarily a bad thing. It gave City's walking wounded more time to recover from injury for the rescheduled date later in the month.

JANUARY 8th

On the day best remembered for Kevin Keegan sensationally quitting as manager of Newcastle, citing difficulties with members of the plc, City chairman Tom Smeaton gave brief details of the prospective share flotation. Although most of it was confidential, he did reveal: "We will not be left behind. We are talking about sooner rather than later."

JANUARY 11th   PREM: Leeds United 3 City 0

A bad day at the office for City as they slumped to a disastrous defeat at Elland Road, and were now fifth bottom in the Premiership. It was so bad that O'Neill went over to City's loyal but disappointed supporters - and apologised. He said afterwards: "It was a desperately poor performance. That was not patronising on my part because I have nothing to be patronising about towards Leicester fans. But they have spent a lot of time and money to travel up to see us and we have been very poor indeed. It was the worst of the season."

JANUARY 15th   FA CUP (3): City 2 (Claridge, Marshall) Southend 0

This comfortable, if unspectacular victory propelled City towards a fourth round confrontation with O'Neill's former club Norwich. Transfer speculation was suddenly rife again, as City were said to have made a £1.5 million bid for Port Vale wingers Steve Guppy and John McCarthy.

JANUARY 16th

City's record transfer fee of £1.25 million, which they paid Notts County for Mark Draper in 1994, was finally broken as Martin O'Neill signed Matt Elliott from Oxford. The fee for the big defender was £1.6 million and O'Neill felt he was worth every penny. Tom Smeaton agreed: "I don't expect the record to last very long. It is going to be broken quite soon, probably." *

Elliott had the choice of City or Southampton - so why Leicester? "The main factor was the enthusiasm of the manager. The other thing was the attraction of the Premiership but basically it came down to his powers of persuasion and I am happy I made the right choice." The fans are all agreed on that Matt!

---

* NB: The transfer record was still intact more than a year later.

Claridge's goals kept flowing as City kept their hopes alive in two Cup competitions.

JANUARY 18th   PREM: City 1 (Heskey) Wimbledon 0
Elliott's debut was a good, solid one as City put on one of their best displays of the season. The new recruit was happy too: "It went very well but the main thing was that the whole team played very well."

JANUARY 21st   COCA-COLA CUP QUARTER-FINAL:
                      Ipswich 0 City 1 (Robins)
Elliott had to sit this one and the rest of the tournament out after representing Oxford in the early rounds, but watched with delight as Mark Robins, back from a loan spell in Copenhagen, scored a fine individual goal to book a semi-final tie with Wimbledon. Robins said: "I went to Denmark on loan and did well there. They've indicated they may want me for next season but I would rather stay in English football with Leicester."

JANUARY 25th   FA CUP (4): City 2 (Marshall, Parker) Norwich 1
Three goals, two sendings off, two penalties and one winner meant this was a typical blood and thunder Cup affair. Neil Lennon saw red after a first half scuffle with an opponent, who also got his marching orders, and Martin O'Neill said despite the result he wasn't overjoyed: "This was not one of our better days. The match at Ipswich had taken more out of us than we had thought but we got through it, just." A home tie with Chelsea would be City's reward.

Meanwhile, Pontus Kaamark faced another lengthy lay off, this time with a broken arm. A possible arrival in the shape of Pieter Huistra didn't materialise as the former Rangers winger failed to impress the City boss in a reserve match.

JANUARY 29th   PREM: City 1 (Parker) Sunderland 1
Two of last season's promoted sides produced a disappointing stalemate at Filbert Street. A debatable penalty rescued City, Garry Parker's fourth, and last goal of the season - all from the penalty spot. City were 13th.

So close to glory

FEBRUARY 2nd   PREM: Newcastle 4 City 3 (Claridge, Elliott, Heskey)
These two sides have been involved in several high scoring matches over the years. Back in 1990, Newcastle were 4-2 down with 12 minutes to go when City were taken apart and lost 5-4, the winner being scored in the dying seconds by a certain Mark McGhee. Later on that year, City gained revenge, winning 5-4 at Filbert Street. Then, in 1993, the Magpies put seven past Leicester on the final day of the season.

This time, once again, there were seven goals, and again there was an amazing finish. City had stormed back after conceding an early goal and led 3-1 thanks to some fine finishing. But with the minutes ticking away, England's number one striker banged in a hat trick, the winner in stoppage time, to break City hearts. Martin

O'Neill couldn't believe it: "Of course it was a crushing disappointment to lose a game in that way. I would have to say it was the most painful defeat I have ever had to suffer as a manager. It is hard to take in."

FEBRUARY 3rd-15th

O'Neill was not impressed by the actions of several un-named players for being drunk and rowdy at a testimonial evening for Steve Walsh. Organiser, and local boxing personality, Johnny Griffin said: "Quite honestly, the behaviour was disgraceful. Steve came up to me afterwards and apologised on their behalf. He deserved better, he's a lovely man." O'Neill's reaction was: "After getting beaten 4-3, you would have hoped they would have kept their mouths shut."

Another one of the players was in trouble too. Neil Lennon appeared before a disciplinary hearing and was found guilty of misconduct, as well as being warned about his future behaviour, for allegedly gesturing to fans during the 2-0 win over Newcastle earlier in the season. O'Neill said: "Hopefully he will have learned a lesson."

Transfer speculation linked O'Neill with former Norwich player Robert Ullathorne, now plying his trade in Spain. Arsenal striker John Hartson was also said to be on his shopping list.

FEBRUARY 16th   FA CUP (5): City 2 (Walsh, own goal) Chelsea 2

Chelsea's foreign legion came to Filbert Street to face a City side depleted by injuries and suspensions. They really were down to the bare bones as first team regulars Elliott, Kaamark, Izzet, Lennon, Heskey, Marshall and Whitlow, plus squad members Hill, Rolling and Lewis were all unavailable. Two goals down, and seemingly out of the tie, City bounced back thanks to Garry Parker and his free kicks; Steve Walsh headed in the first and Eddie Newton deflected the ball into his own net with only moments remaining to equalise. Rousing stuff for the crowd and BBC television viewers, marred by some fighting amongst fans.

Chelsea boss Ruud Gullit infuriated O'Neill by calling City 'lucky' and was not impressed by their long ball and set piece tactics. A very angry O'Neill snapped: "This was a Cup tie and you get through it any way you can with the resources available to you. Before the game I would have settled for a draw, but at half time I would have settled for a corner."

FEBRUARY 17th

City eventually signed Robert Ullathorne from Osasuna for £600,000. The player, who was with O'Neill at Norwich, told the press conference: "I'm just happy to be here. Leicester City are a great club, they are doing well in the league and are still in the two Cup competitions. I enjoyed my spell in Spain but I wanted to play in the best league in the world - the Premiership." Ullathorne was included in the City team for the Cup semi-final 24 hours later, a debut he would never forget.

FEBRUARY 18th   COCA-COLA CUP SEMI-FINAL 1st leg:
                     City 0 Wimbledon 0

See next chapter

Scotland and Wales (yeah, right!) do battle – but Elliott has the last laugh.

FEBRUARY 20th

The *Daily Mirror* reported that Pontus Kaamark was not impressed with some of his colleagues. The Swedish international was quoted as saying: "We get to training some mornings and I am sure some of the players are going to drop out because of what happened the night before. I wouldn't be able to get out of bed for days if I had been that drunk." O'Neill's reaction was one of surprise: "His remarks, if he did indeed make them, certainly do not refer to anything during my time here."

Kaamark, who is as close to teetotal as you can get, was fuming: "When I saw the papers I couldn't believe it. The whole thing was not true. I never said any of the things and I am very upset at the situation." O'Neill added: "I have told the players that if they are drinking every night and still manage to get such good results, I'll be out there joining them!"

Marshall stunner

FEBRUARY 22nd   PREM: City 4 (Marshall 3, Claridge) Derby County 2

After going behind to an early goal, City destroyed the old enemy thanks to a blistering Marshall hat trick. The result lifted not only the players but the fans too who were in need of a convincing home display. O'Neill: "It's all about points and it was a big psychological boost to get to the 30 mark. I think 42 points will be safe and we still have work to do to get them."

FEBRUARY 26th   FA CUP (5) REPLAY: Chelsea 1 City 0 (AET)

A night to be proud as a City supporter but also a night that brings back such a nasty memory. A quality, battling display against the stylish West Londoners took them into extra time where only a controversial decision prevented City from reaching the penalty shoot-out and a possible place in the quarter finals. With two minutes remaining, Erland Johnsen hurled himself into the box and conned referee Mike Reed into awarding a foul. Frank Leboeuf made no mistake from the penalty spot. City's management team, the players, City fans, the watching TV pundits, the armchair supporters and so on could not believe it. Every time you saw the replay, it looked less and less a penalty and made you more and more angry.

No-one was more distraught than the manager. O'Neill lashed out: "I think the referee should maybe take a long hard look at his performance in this game. It's scandalous that a team should be put out of the competition in this way because of a totally wrong decision, and the frustrating thing is we can do nothing about it." He added: "It is quite unbelievable. The referee was just five yards away and missed it completely. My defenders tell me that Johnsen was not touched. It's not sour grapes, honestly, and in a couple of weeks time it won't matter. I am not saying we would have won the tie but I think we deserved the chance to be at least in the penalty shoot-out.

"I think we would have been better off losing in the third round than to go out in such a disgraceful manner," claimed O'Neill.

FEBRUARY 28th
O'Neill cheered himself up by spending some of the club's money on Steve Guppy, a winger who played for him at Wycombe. A brief spell at Newcastle followed, then he signed for Port Vale where he excelled and helped persuade O'Neill to part with £850,000. O'Neill revealed: "This is not the last piece of the jigsaw. It is never completed and, if someone else is available and in our price range, we will still try to sign him."

Meanwhile, O'Neill learned that no action was to be taken over his comments following the Chelsea replay. He also stated that he didn't want to see video replays assisting referees. The referee who so incensed O'Neill, Mike Reed, was appointed to take charge of the Chelsea-City match in March, but even though City made no objection, the FA later changed their mind. Reed, too, changed his mind when he saw the Johnsen incident on Sky: "Last night the TV cameras showed it from a different angle and there wasn't any contact. But, from where I was, there was."

MARCH 1st   PREM: Wimbledon 1 City 3 (Elliott 2, Robins)
This was the second meeting between the two in the space of a few weeks and it was here at Selhurst Park where we got a glimpse of Matt Elliott's attacking qualities, scoring two fine goals. City moved up to 10th and O'Neill said: "As far as being in the top half of the table is concerned, right now positions don't mean anything. It is the points total that is important and we have not got to the 42 point mark yet."

MARCH 4th
Prime Minister John Major, speaking on *BBC Radio Five Live*, was asked about the Chelsea-Leicester game and in particular the controversial penalty. Mr Major, a Chelsea fan, said: "I'm afraid I do not think it was a penalty. In the harsh glare of TV close ups he was wrong but it was a pretty crowded penalty area." That makes it alright then does it?

Meanwhile, a group of City fans announced they were to sue the FA over the penalty decision, but this turned out to be a publicity stunt.

MARCH 5th   PREM: City 1 (Claridge) Aston Villa 0
Brian Little's jinx against City continued when Steve Claridge, once of Villa's near neighbours Birmingham, scored the only goal to keep their good run going. The win moved City upto ninth place and made relegation look a million miles away. O'Neill was very happy: "Once again, the spirit of the side was excellent."

Midfielder Garry Parker played despite his wife being in hospital with their baby, being born four months prematurely, fighting for its life. O'Neill allowed Parker to have a mobile phone on the bench in case of any news. Parker said: "We are going from minute to minute."

Before the match, Brian Little perhaps surprised City fans when he said: "Supporters may not believe it but I actually have a soft spot for Leicester and I am very pleased to see them doing so well." However, a storm erupted that night when Mark McGhee took offence to comments O'Neill made. O'Neill praised Little's record at Filbert Street and added: ". . . what you wish to do when Mark McGhee visits us with Wolves is entirely at your own discretion . . ."

McGhee, quoted in the *Leicester Mercury*, stormed: "I will take legal advice. He seems to be encouraging some sort of divide." The League Managers Association looked into the matter and said that O'Neill's remarks were "meant to be taken lightheartedly" and they would take no action.

MARCH 8th   PREM: Coventry 0 City 0

City's dismal run of results over 20 years at Highfield Road continued but they did at least earn a point this time. With 37 in the bag and 10 games to go, a comfortable end to the season was in prospect. If only football were that simple. O'Neill: "We thought that we played well without a cutting edge but we are not out of the woods yet."

MARCH 11th   COCA-COLA CUP Semi-final 2nd leg:
                    Wimbledon 1 City 1 (Grayson)
                    Agg 1-1 (City win on the away goals rule)

See next chapter

MARCH 14th

Garry Parker, still bravely playing despite family difficulties, came off the transfer list, at his own request. O'Neill was delighted: "That's good news because he's presently producing the best form I have seen from him since I became manager here."

MARCH 15th   PREM: City 1 (Marshall) Middlesbrough 3

A dress rehearsal for the forthcoming Coca-Cola Cup Final turned into a nightmare for City as they were torn apart by Juninho and co. in the first half. Marshall's early goal after the re-start gave them hope but they couldn't build on it. Despite the defeat, Martin O'Neill saw things which helped him pick a team for the Wembley showdown three weeks later.

He said: "Juninho was just coming into form and we had him watched for a couple of weeks. We knew that really he needed to be man marked. I deliberated the night before, shall we stick someone on him? But I decided to let the players have their head. I thought the euphoria of getting through to the final might carry them along and we might just have won the game without man marking, which I don't really like to do. They destroyed us, and any notion of leaving Juninho to run free was well and truly put in its place. In hindsight, I am pleased that he murdered us in that game - it didn't cost us relegation, and it made me re-plan for the Final." He also described their defending as 'naive' and added: "Naive is a euphemism for stupid."

MARCH 18th

City strengthened their goalkeeping department by signing Ian Andrews on a months loan. Andrews, who played for City in the mid 1980s, was brought in as cover for Keller and Poole.

MARCH 19th   PREM: City 1 (Claridge) Tottenham 1

A win would all but have guaranteed City's place in the Premiership and they were heading for all three points until Teddy Sheringham grabbed a last minute equaliser.

Hey lads, Wembley is that way . . .

It left a frustrated O'Neill to reflect: "We had beaten Wimbledon, Derby and Villa before drawing with Coventry . . . 10 points which had taken us from 27 to 37. Then Garry Parker makes an absolute hogs of a pass against Spurs when he should have been trying for Row Z. They equalise late on when three points would have seen us just about safe. I said to him 'If those two points cost us, I'm going to kill you'. I think there was a feeling amongst the players that they were already safe. No, we weren't okay and it is a hard thing to keep people focused all the time."

MARCH 22nd   PREM: Southampton 2 City 2 (Heskey, own goal)
The last match before the Cup Final and a chance for players to impress the manager. Twice City were behind and twice they drew level thanks to some scrambles inside the Southampton penalty area. Initially, Steve Claridge was credited with a goal but that was later taken off him in favour of an own goal. City were proving very hard to beat. In fact, of their last 17 matches, in all competitions, they'd only lost three times. (I know how much Martin enjoys these kind of statistics!) The point at The Dell took City to 39.

With a break before the Cup Final, O'Neill took the players off to Spain but Claridge was conspicuous by his absence. The manager explained why: "Apparently he has some sort of reaction in really hot sun, or so he tells me, so there was no point in taking the risk."

O'Neill, who still had to discuss a new contract with the chairman at this point, was delighted to hear that their final opponents Middlesbrough, had lost their High Court appeal. They were trying to overturn a decision to dock them three points for not fulfilling a fixture. Boro's three point loss obviously helped City in their battle to avoid relegation.

Transfer deadline day, meanwhile, at the end of March passed without significance as far as City were concerned. With no Premiership action to worry City, they could concentrate fully on their assault on the Coca-Cola Cup. Drama? Just a bit!

Success goes to Martin's head . . . allegedly!

CHAPTER EIGHT:

COCA-COLA: IT'S THE REAL THING!

FEBRUARY 18th   COCA-COLA CUP SEMI-FINAL FIRST LEG
                      City 0 Wimbledon 0

Despite the scoreline, City fans would have been happy with this. No goals conceded at home in this kind of Cup tie is always a bonus especially with so much at stake. However, debutant Robert Ullathorne lasted only 12 minutes before suffering a broken leg which would keep him out of action for most of the year. Having signed him the day before, O'Neill said Ullathorne had suffered the worst possible start to his City career: "It's dreadful news. Here he was, just back from Spain, looking forward to the Premiership with us, had one training session, and I thought was playing very well for us. Then, in a freak accident, he has suffered a fracture after just 12 minutes." Of the game itself, just five shots on target tells its own story but O'Neill took comfort from the result: "We are very much in this tie and again you cannot question our spirit and our character."

Garry Parker arrived at Filbert Street less than an hour before kick off due to his wife being in hospital and O'Neill said: "It was a brave decision. Because his wife was with friends and family he felt he could take part in the game. I have to say he played very well indeed."

O'Neill blasts out warning to his players

MARCH 11th   COCA-COLA CUP SEMI-FINAL SECOND LEG
                   Wimbledon 1 City 1 (Grayson) AET
                   (Agg 1-1, City win on away goals)

A night of drama at Selhurst Park watched by thousands of travelling City supporters. After going behind to Marcus Gayle's first half strike, City fought back with Simon Grayson their unlikely hero, heading in at the far post from Parker's free kick.

Parker was then hero himself at the other end clearing off the line as the Dons piled forward in extra time. City hung on, courtesy of the away goals rule, and booked yet another trip to Wembley. Grayson's goal, a rarity for the utility player, especially with his head, knew full well what it meant to everyone: "The goals don't come very often and I have no doubt that it was the most important goal I've scored in my career. We had a bit of luck there but that's what you need sometime. We didn't get any at Chelsea and it's swings and roundabouts."

"That was the longest 120 minutes of my life," revealed O'Neill. "I don't know how old I was at the beginning but I am 93 now! It was a great effort by all the players and a great effort by the supporters as well. It makes up for a lot of the disappointment from the Chelsea game and we are all absolutely delighted." City's opponents were confirmed 24 hours later when even though Middlesbrough lost 1-0 at home to Stockport, they won on aggregate 2-1.

SUNDAY APRIL 6th @ WEMBLEY – COCA-COLA CUP FINAL
Middlesbrough 1 City 1 (Heskey) AET

A glorious, sunny day at Wembley was the setting for what turned out to be a far from classic League Cup Final. Beforehand, skipper Steve Walsh knew that despite being underdogs, City had an advantage: "Unlike Boro, we still have a lot of players here who have experienced Wembley and that could be to our benefit." As ever, Martin O'Neill was a pre-match optimist: "This time, to win the competition is everything. I have won the Cup as a player and I have lost it too, and that is not a good day."

Garry Parker entered the game looking to win a fourth winners medal but he was just delighted to be playing: "I honestly thought I would never play at Wembley again after the Palace match." Parker's goal against Palace took the play-off final into extra time 11 months previous before Steve Claridge 'shinned' the winner. But could the journeyman striker do it again? He said: "It would be great to think so. Who would have thought we would be back at Wembley so soon? If it was a choice between staying up or winning the cup, I would choose staying up every time. Anything else will be a bonus - but I'll be trying my hardest to win."

O'Neill's decision to use Pontus Kaamark as a man marker for Juninho worked a treat in keeping the little Brazilian quiet. Even though Heskey and Ravanelli both hit the woodwork in normal time, an extra half hour was required. Boro's £42,000 a week Italian fired Bryan Robson's team into the lead but, once again, City drew on all their strength to snatch a draw at the death. Mark Robins, City's quarter final hero, crossed to the far post where Steve Walsh knocked the ball to Heskey. His header came back off the bar and Claridge saw his shot saved. Fortunately, Heskey was on hand to bundle the ball over the line. 'Oh, what drama' to quote a famous piece of radio commentary from May 1994.

O'Neill was both delighted and relieved by the last gasp intervention from Heskey and was quick to pay tribute to his players: "We never gave up. I thought that epitomised us, that never-say-die spirit and the goal came even when I thought the lads' efforts were waning. We live to fight another day." Wembley veteran Steve Walsh added: "We have shown that we have the spirit not to give up and we feel great that we have managed to save ourselves at the death. If it goes down to the wire next time, then we will be ready again."

The outstanding Muzzy Izzet leaves Emerson in his wake.

Hero Heskey sends the 35,000 blue and white half of Wembley crazy.

It's there! A great feeling as City leave it late at Wembley – yet again.

WEDNESDAY APRIL 16th @ HILLSBOROUGH
COCA-COLA CUP FINAL REPLAY
Middlesbrough 0 City 1 (Claridge) AET

Like the first game, it was goalless after 90 tense, nervous minutes and again it was not one for the neutrals. Ten minutes into extra time and City were awarded a free kick which Parker floated in towards Walsh. The captain headed it down into the path of Claridge who swivelled to fire into the back of the net. Cue scenes of mayhem both on and off the pitch. The fans were ecstatic, O'Neill did his usual trick of jumping into orbit and everyone looked at their watches to see how long was left; 20 minutes. Immediately Boro fought back but Kasey Keller made an outstanding save from Emerson to keep City's noses in front. Everyone around me at Hillsborough sat or stood with fingers crossed praying for full time. It seemed like hours.

STEVIE WONDER

Then came the final whistle. They had done it. They had won the cup. They had qualified for Europe. It was hard to take in. Everybody was gripped by emotion. Some were in tears. Some were silent trying to make sense of it all. Some danced. Some waved flags. Many sang. Some hugged complete strangers. But at the end of it all, it was their most amazing achievement for a long, long time. Not many supporters under 40 would remember the last League Cup success three and a half decades ago. Remarkable stuff.

So Claridge repeated the trick to give City glory and he was almost lost for words: "Marvellous, just marvellous. I didn't shin this one! Who says lightening never strikes twice? I never back myself to score first, if I had done, I would have missed. It's a dream come true." He added: "Europe, eh? We could all be going to Barcelona. It would really faze them running out at Filbert Street, you know, seeing the East Stand!!"

"What a 12 months for Steve Claridge," beamed O'Neill. "I'm going to get absolutely lambasted with a few glasses of wine. I do feel sorry for Bryan Robson as Boro played some very good football. But I thought we deserved to win. We showed passion and desire." He added: "To qualify for Europe means just about everything, but tonight is about winning the Coca-Cola Cup. It is magnificent - the most magnificent 15 months of my life. When I came here, we couldn't get a result in the first 10 games and it has been well documented that the natives were restless - and tonight they were restless for a different reason. Now we're in Europe. Can you believe it?"

Man of the match Walsh probably thought that his winning goal at Wembley against Derby in 1994 would be the highlight of a distinguished City career. Then came Wembley 1996, now this. "This is without doubt the high point and it is a tremendous feeling. Definitely the proudest moment of my life. When I looked around and saw all our fans, I felt we had to do it for them. They were marvellous and I am delighted we were able to win it for them. It's just fantastic. The icing on the cake was winning the man of the match award. That, and my medal, made it a special night all round for me."

Although Claridge grabbed the headlines, defender Simon Grayson felt Kasey Keller deserved as much credit: "Looking back I think his save from Emerson was the moment when the Cup was ours. It was a tremendous save."

The final word on the replay win comes from Garry Parker, who summed up everyone's feelings when he described the impact Martin O'Neill had made in his time with Leicester. "When he came here just over halfway through last season, he came in for some criticism. But he turned it round and got us in the Premiership, and now we have taken it on to win the Cup. It is unbelievable." He continued: "I've been at big clubs like Forest and Villa in the past, but, as clubs go, this is just unbelievable team spirit; the manager, the coaches, it's all just one big family."

What a fantastic achievement; simply amazing. But O'Neill the magician still had one more rabbit to pull out of his hat - Premiership safety. If he could do that, as well as winning silverware and getting City into Europe, the doubters would surely be no more.

Man of the Match (Walsh) and matchwinner (Claridge) are agreed:
Coca-Cola – It's The Real Thing!

BLOODY HELL FRANK! THIS IS THE 379TH PHOTO I'VE TAKEN
OF YOU AND THAT PILKINGTON CUP THINGY!!

CHAPTER NINE:

WHAT DIFFERENCE DOES IT MAKE?

APRIL 6th   COCA-COLA CUP FINAL see previous chapter

APRIL 9th   PREM: Everton 1 City 1 (Marshall)
Just a few days after the Coca-Cola Cup final, City reshuffled the pack for the trip to Goodison. Back came Guppy, Elliott and Marshall and it was the latter, a Merseysider through and through, who rescued a point in the second half for City. So 40 points in the bag, and Martin O'Neill was still urging a note of caution: "We want 42 points to be certain but I will sit down and have a long hard look at it and see if I can work the whole thing out."

APRIL 12th   PREM: Arsenal 2 City 0
With the Cup replay in the coming week, O'Neill changed the team around again resting Kaamark, Prior, Walsh, Parker and Heskey, and he left Claridge and Izzet on the bench. This emphasised he was keeping something in reserve for the replay. Arsenal were clear winners, a fact not lost on O'Neill: "We did not play at all well. We were second best through out."

APRIL 13th
Emile Heskey's rise to fame continued when he was recognised in the PFA awards. He came second in the Young Player category, beaten only by Manchester United superstar David Beckham.

APRIL 16th   COCA-COLA CUP FINAL REPLAY see previous chapter

APRIL 19th   PREM: Chelsea 2 City 1 (own goal)
This was City's first match after being crowned Coca-Cola Cup winners. Before kick off, the Chelsea players gave City bouquets of flowers to mark their achievement. But you suspect they were a bit of a peace offering after the FA Cup penalty rumpus the previous month. City had chances to get a point here with Marshall especially unlucky not to head an equaliser. The fight for safety continued and O'Neill said: "I won't say it was a hangover but I did know it was going to be hard to get the players to show the same intensity they had done the other night."

Praying for Premiership survival. Martin seems well connected with 'Him' upstairs, doesn't he?

APRIL 23rd　　　　　**PREM: City 0 West Ham 1**

Three Premiership defeats on the trot plunged City into relegation trouble even though their 40 points could be enough in itself to stave off the drop. This match was a dull, uneventful affair with a scrappy John Moncur goal separating the two sides. Three games to go for City - it was getting all too close at the bottom. O'Neill was putting a brave face on things: "At best, the issue is still in our own hands. I think we might need to win one more game to be absolutely sure. Even though we have done a lot better than everyone expected, the Premiership is still hard for us."

APRIL 28th

Steve Walsh laid out his intentions about the future; he desperately wants to see out his career at Filbert Street. He revealed: "Nothing has been discussed yet. My main priority is to get the points we need to stay up. If I get the right offer, I will stay." Meanwhile, a bumper crowd of over 13,000 turned out for Walshie's testimonial match which included former City players as well as many big names in the football world such as Paul Gascoigne. Gazza's mate Chris Evans joined in as well.

MAY 3rd　　　　　**PREM: City 2 (Walsh, Marshall) Manchester United 2**

A win for City would have clinched Premiership survival but they had to settle for a point against the Champions-elect. The match was eloquently described by *The Fox* fanzine, who wrote:

"If you are looking for one moment that summed up the adventures of the Unlikely Lads during the glorious 96-97 season, then this is as good as any. On a sunny Saturday morning in May, Manchester United, without doubt the best side in the country, came to Filbert Street and by the 20th minute of the game found themselves 2-0 down as City took them apart. The second goal, which came from Ian Marshall, who looks more like a farmer or a gardener than a Premiership striker, was a beauty. That United rescued a point is less important than the fact that it was City who were pressing for a winner and came within a whisker on a number of occasions. It was in stark contrast to United's last Premiership visit when a side packed with reserves humiliated City 4-0, and it could quite easily have been 7-0. This time though, City proved that they could live on the same pitch as the champions."

Despite the performance, other results saw them slip to fifth from bottom. The heat had been most definitely turned up. O'Neill said: "We showed we can play a bit, and, delightfully, the matter still rests in our own hands, that's the main thing. Before the game maybe we would have settled for a point and I have to say that, even at 2-0 up, I never felt all that comfortable against a side like United. In the end a point is a fine result for us. Our attitude was spot on."

MAY 4th

In the annual Supporters Club award ceremony at Filbert Street, members voted for Simon Grayson as their Player of the Year, the second time he'd won the award in recent seasons. Emerging prospect Stuart Campbell was named Young Player, and Steve Claridge's Coca-Cola Cup fourth round volley against Manchester United was voted Goal of the Season.

No panic here

MAY 7th   PREM: City 1 (Elliott) Sheffield Wednesday 0
With less than 10 minutes to go and the game scoreless, it seemed that City would
have to make the journey to Ewood Park on the final day of the season still sweating
on their Premiership future. Then, step forward Matt Elliott to blast the ball home, his
fourth goal since joining in January. It was without doubt the most important as it
secured the club's top flight status for another 12 months at least. He said: "It was a
difficult game as it was all a bit tense, but I never thought that we would lose. As far
as the goal went, I just thought to myself 'go for it'. It was a bit of a miskick but it
went in, and that's the main thing."

MAY 11th PREM: Blackburn 2 City 4
(Heskey 2, Wilson, Claridge)
A fairly meaningless contest between
two sides who had already secured
their safety turned out to be an
entertaining one as City slammed in
four goals, for their joint biggest win
of the season. Martin O'Neill left his
backroom staff in charge as he sat up in
the directors box at Ewood Park. The
victory propelled City upto the dizzy
heights of ninth in the table, a superb
end to the season and one which few
could have predicted back in August.

So the following campaign will no
doubt be one where City are
challenging for the title, a European
trophy and both domestic Cup
competitions then? Er, no, not
according to O'Neill: "Just in case
anyone gets carried away, the target is
just the same and I know next season
that the pressure will be on us to do
better. I don't think there has been a
team in the Premiership who have
worked harder than us," he admitted.
And it's difficult to argue with that
opinion.

Phew! What a season!!

CHAPTER TEN:

YOU'VE GOT EVERYTHING NOW

MAY 1997

As soon as the campaign had drawn to a close, Martin O'Neill was already focussing on the season to come. But the main thing occupying supporters' minds was the future of a man who had dramatically made the club great again. O'Neill still had a year to go on his original contract and fans were beginning to wonder if the so-called 'big clubs' would come calling his name. Two days after the Blackburn game, O'Neill told the *Leicester Mercury*: "I am perfectly happy to stick with the original length of contract, which has another season to go. I said when I came here I would not be leaving unless it was the club's decision to get rid of me and that still stands.

"Who knows, if we have a bad start to next season, they might want to sack me." O'Neill may have impressed us and most of the footballing world, but Alex Ferguson was crowned Manager of the Year after leading Manchester United to another championship title, as well as the European Cup semi-finals. However, both O'Neill and Wimbledon's Joe Kinnear were singled out for special mention. Chairman Tom Smeaton joined in the O'Neill debate by issuing a 'hands-off' warning to any club interested in prising him away from the Filbert Street hotseat. Everton, Southampton and Celtic were all linked with him.

Meanwhile, Emile Heskey scored his first goal for his country as England Under 21s drew 1-1 with Poland. And Northern Ireland international Neil Lennon was said to be one of Chelsea's transfer targets, something O'Neill denied. One player who left in May was out of contract Frank Rolling, who eventually joined Bournemouth. And surprise, surprise, the club increased the price of season tickets by up to 13%.

Hands off O'Neill

JUNE/JULY

The start of the month was a good one for City supporters as Martin O'Neill decided to pledge his immediate future to the club. He signed a three-year deal to keep him at

Filbert Street until the year 2000. Chairman Tom Smeaton echoed the supporters' feelings when he said: "This is great news. He is one of the most talented managers in the country and the fact that he has committed himself to Leicester City for another three years demonstrates his confidence in the club." After some deliberation about signing the contract extension, O'Neill looked forward to the future with optimism:

"I am hoping the new deal, which gives me an extra two years, will give the club a platform to keep the momentum of the previous 18 months going. And we are obviously hoping to establish ourselves firmly in the Premiership which we all know becomes increasingly difficult every year." The club also revealed that they'd rejected a number of multi-million pound bids for their star striker Emile Heskey.

Also staying at Filbert Street was inspirational skipper Steve Walsh, who signed a new two-year deal. As far as O'Neill was concerned, he never wanted Walsh to go: "His character and determination have been invaluable to us since I came here. He is going to be important to the team, even if he doesn't play in every game." Walsh, too, was excited about the future: "I am delighted to be staying at Leicester but to be honest I never even thought about going anywhere else. Last season was magnificent. Now I'm really looking forward to the future here."

Garry Parker sorted out his future, despite press stories which stirred up a bit of conflict between the player and the club. Parker's decision to stay and the arrival of Robbie Savage (22) from Crewe for £400,000 strengthened the battle for midfield places, but O'Neill pulled out of a deal which could have seen Norwich's Andy Johnson coming to Filbert Street. Savage was a former team-mate of Neil Lennon and was excited about the move: "Leicester are a hard working team and that is one thing I do, I give 100%. I have seen how well Neil has done here. If I do half as well as that, then I will be fine."

Three City stalwarts ended their long association with the club; Colin Hill and Kevin Poole both took up the option of free transfers. Hill went to Sweden before returning to play for Northampton, and Poole, who lives in Bromsgrove, got a deal nearer to home at Birmingham. The big departure of the summer came as a shock to the fans, and an even bigger shock to Martin O'Neill. Out of contract Simon Grayson re-joined the man who brought him to Filbert Street, Brian Little, over at Aston Villa. The fee was eventually agreed at £1.35 million; Not bad for someone who cost just £50,000 in 1992. O'Neill was amazed, as he felt Grayson was about to sign a new deal: "I thought it was just a matter of dotting the i's and crossing the t's. This has come totally out of the blue. I am very disappointed but if a player wants to join another club that's his prerogative."

Grayson, twice named as fans' Player of the Year, enjoyed a chequered career with City. Initially a supporters favourite which culminated in lifting the play-off trophy at Wembley, Grayson suffered a dip in form and was barracked mercilessly. Then he improved quite considerably and the fans loved him again. The fickle face of football, eh? So, any regrets? He said: "I've got a lot of great friends in Leicester and I really enjoyed my five years, and am attached to the area. But the ambition and the size of Villa meant I had to take the chance. I feel I was a good servant to the club and I hope people won't forget that."

Also on the move, but on a lesser scale, were Jamie Lawrence to Bradford for £50,000 and Neil Lewis to Peterborough for £60,000.

*O'Neill gets his message across as City
began the season well.*

City ended July in Greece to play a pre-season match against Olympiakos. The 3-1 defeat was compounded by some frightening scenes as bottles and coins were hurled at the City bench during the match. O'Neill, as you can imagine, was none too impressed: "I was serious about calling the game off. The game itself served its purpose and it takes our preparation forward a bit."

EARLY AUGUST
With Kevin Poole's decision to leave, City needed cover for Kasey Keller and they opted to sign Frenchman Pegguy Arphexad, who looked good while on trial. His arrival was overshadowed by that of Graham Fenton, who scored his last goal for Blackburn AGAINST City on the final day of last season. The £1.1 million transfer was done 48 hours before the big kick off and Fenton was glad to leave Ewood Park: "It was clear that I was not part of Roy Hodgson's plans and I desperately wanted first team football." The addition of Fenton to the squad proved to be great timing as, 24 hours later, midfielder Scott Taylor broke down in training, suffering a ruptured kneecap tendon that would prevent him playing all season.

Despite this, City entered the new campaign with a lot more pressure on the shoulders of Martin O'Neill. Could he inspire the players to do it again? Or would they be one season wonders?

When the fixture list was revealed, Martin O'Neill's reaction was "It's a tough start" and his views echoed those of most of us. Aston Villa, Liverpool, Manchester United and Arsenal are without doubt four of the biggest clubs in England and O'Neill hoped they would get through that without too much damage. Three or maybe four points wouldn't be a bad return considering the opposition. And the bookmakers had little faith in City again, with some tipping them for relegation along with the likes of promoted Barnsley.

AUGUST 9th   PREM: City 1 (Marshall) Aston Villa 0
O'Neill's first team selection was as unpredictable as it was imaginative. Stuart Campbell was rewarded for his excellent pre-season form with a starting place and on the bench was more than £3 million worth of talent. New signings Savage and Fenton were joined by Parker and Claridge, the latter losing out to Ian Marshall up front. Marshall repaid the manager's faith with the only goal against a team who would represent England, alongside City, in the U.E.F.A. Cup. The result also continued Brian Little's hoodoo against his former club. Five matches, two draws and three wins for City must really get up Little's nose! O'Neill couldn't hide his delight at the display, as well as the win:

"When you looked at the fixtures you might have wondered where the first point was coming from but we are off the mark and that's the important thing."

AUGUST 13th   PREM: Liverpool 1 City 2 (Elliott, Fenton)
City again stunned their illustrious opponents with a goal after just 72 seconds; Matt Elliott catching Liverpool on the hop to give City a flying start. Substitute Fenton silenced the Anfield crowd (there were no City fans allocated tickets although a few did get in here and there) before Paul Ince pulled one back to make them sweat in the closing stages. The result put City fourth with two victories and O'Neill was jubilant:

"We were absolutely magnificent. We didn't come here to be rolled over and I would say we deserved the win. That's six points, Liverpool have one." And he added: "I say now that I would settle for being two points BEHIND them at the end of the season!"

MID AUGUST

Former West Ham and Everton striker Tony Cottee was added to the City squad after completing a half million pound transfer. His spell in Malaysia was not as happy as he'd hoped. Meanwhile, new recruit Robbie Savage did his reputation no harm at all scoring a wonderful goal for his country, even though Wales were stuffed by Turkey 6-3.

AUGUST 23rd   PREM: City 0 Manchester United 0

City's 100% start to the season may have come to an end but their amazing run continued as they held the champions at Filbert Street - and stopped them scoring. Midfielder Neil Lennon, whose last goal came at Old Trafford back in November 1996, said: "We have showed that we are a decent side, capable of playing good football." O'Neill singled out Elliott for another stunning defensive performance: "I thought he was absolutely terrific. I knew he could play at this level. He reads the game so well."

AUGUST 27th   PREM: City 3 (Heskey, Elliott, Walsh) Arsenal 3

A brilliant hat trick from the equally brilliant Dennis Bergkamp still couldn't deny City a share of the spoils. In a match which the Gunners dominated up to the last few minutes, City showed the sort of determination and belief which O'Neill has instilled into the players. At two goals down with more than 80 minutes gone, some fans trooped out of the ground disappointed, but having seen an Arsenal team that were a little bit special. What they missed was breathtaking.

First, Heskey scrambled in what we thought was a consolation; Elliott pushed himself forward and scored what we thought was a 90th minute equaliser; Then Bergkamp completed his treble to score what we thought was the winner; But hold on. Enter the captain. Walsh heads it in. And it's 3-3. And we thought that was that. The final whistle did blow straight after but the action didn't cease, as Arsenal players surrounded the referee to complain about the six minutes of time added on. An altercation followed, but it was all tame stuff. However, Walsh, Ian Wright (who had run 60 yards from the bench), Patrick Viera and coach Pat Rice were all reported to the FA. Martin O'Neill's reaction was: "I didn't see what happened exactly. It was such a dramatic end to the game and obviously feelings were running high, but as a captain he (Walsh) is supposed to set an example and I will be having a word with him."

Of the rather extra-ordinary game, Elliott said: "We never know when we are beaten. We looked dead and buried but we just kept plugging away and put pressure on them." City remained fourth with eight points from those four tough fixtures.

AUGUST 29th

As Emile Heskey was called in to Glenn Hoddle's England squad for the World Cup qualifier with Moldova, City learned of their first round opponents in the UEFA Cup.

They were paired with Juninho's new team, Atletico Madrid, ironically the same opponents they faced in European competition in the early 1960s. O'Neill said: "I thought when Juninho went off to Spain we had seen the last of him! It's a fantastic draw and at least it guarantees a big crowd at Filbert Street."

Off the field, the club warned supporters about the dangers of 'pirate' organisations offering travel to Spain. Quoted in the local press, club spokesman Paul Mice said: "As the capacity is 80,000, we would hope that we would be able to satisfy every supporter wanting to make the journey." 'Satisfy' is an interesting word isn't it?

AUGUST 30th   PREM: Sheffield Wednesday 1 City 0

If, several weeks prior to this, you were asked to name one match in the first five which you thought City would be most likely to win, this would have been it. But seasoned City followers know that history says they beat the big teams and struggle against the others. This was no different as City lost to a far from impressive Wednesday side; Carbone winning, then scoring the penalty. O'Neill: "It would have been nice to have looked towards the two-week break coming up with at least another point to have kept the unbeaten run going."

EARLY SEPTEMBER

Already supporters were complaining about the ticket arrangements for the trip to Atletico Madrid. This proved to be nothing compared to what actually happened.

SEPTEMBER 13th   PREM: City 3 (Walsh, Guppy, Heskey) Tottenham 0

This result took City back to fifth and had O'Neill looking for the right superlative to use: "We were brilliant and excellent and I am ecstatic, the usual - and something which surprised the players, I actually told them!" O'Neill deflected speculation linking out of favour Steve Claridge with a move away from Filbert Street by saying: "I did receive an enquiry, however the main point is I am not interested in letting my best players go at the moment. In fact, when Steve came on for the closing stages, I saw signs of the old Claridge. He is definitely not out of the picture."

So this comprehensive victory set City up nicely for their European adventure, which turned out to be unforgettable in many ways.

CHAPTER ELEVEN:

NOWHERE FAST

SEPTEMBER 16TH   UEFA CUP FIRST ROUND FIRST LEG
Atletico Madrid 2 City 1 (Marshall)

City in Europe! Only supporters with very long memories could claim to have tasted this before. The match itself was overshadowed in many ways as fans were disgracefully treated on route to the ground. Once inside the magnificent Vicente Calderon stadium, the City supporters were celebrating almost straight away as Ian Marshall crashed the ball home from close range to give them a shock 11th minute lead. Soon after, Marshall was badly injured and had to be stretchered off but City managed to keep a tight ship and Claridge went close just before half time. City held out until late on when Madrid scored twice, including a debatable penalty. A 2-1 defeat on the night was certainly no disgrace, a point acknowledged by O'Neill:

"We will roll up our sleeves for the return leg and we are in with a great chance. The away goal is going to be so important. Overall, the team were magnificent. We have done absolutely brilliantly, scored an away goal and looked competitive against a top class team." Of the penalty, he said: "When the guy went down it was inevitable."

Steve Guppy, who conceded the spot-kick, was clearly infuriated: "He just ran into the area and fell over. The penalty award was unlucky." Skipper Steve Walsh added: "The tie is far from over but we have it all to do at Filbert Street." And goal hero Marshall said: "On the face of it, the result is a good one for us, but we feel disappointed not to have won from the position we were in."

SEPTEMBER 18th

A meeting of the Football Association's disciplinary committee decided on leniency over the fracas at the end of City's recent game with Arsenal. Steve Walsh was cleared of serious misconduct but was warned about his future behaviour. Martin O'Neill's reaction was: "The phrase 'storm in a teacup' has been bandied about and that is still it for me."

SEPTEMBER 19th

Defender Mike Whitlow, unable to hold down a regular first team place, was on the move. The former Leeds full back, who spent five and a half years at Filbert Street, joined Bolton for £700,000. O'Neill said: "The move is right for the club and the player. We wish him well."

Never-say-die Neil Lennon wins this duel with Madrid's Kiko.

SEPTEMBER 20th   PREM: Leeds 0 City 1 (Walsh)

Steve Walsh followed in the footsteps of Ian Marshall by scoring, then going off injured. His 31st minute header was the only goal of a rather dull game, but it did lift City into the Premiership's top three, more unchartered territory explored by the seemingly unstoppable Martin O'Neill.

Steve Claridge, who started in Spain but failed to make even the subs bench at Elland Road, was not happy. But O'Neill said: "No-one has a divine right to be in the team. I would like to see him fighting for his place."

Off the field, the club had become embroiled in a public relations disaster as supporters revealed how bad the trip to Spain was, organised by City themselves. According to fans, the coach journey was a nightmare and one said: "We were treated like animals." Others had similar stories. Even the Foreign Office stepped in to investigate. City's offer of a £35 gift voucher as a goodwill gesture was not widely welcomed as it had to be spent in the club's OWN stores.

SEPTEMBER 24th   City 1 (Izzet) Blackburn 1

This draw and other results dropped City one place to fourth, still a fantastic position, if not a fantastic match. Both goals were pretty special, including a rare strike from Muzzy Izzet, a player who just gets better and better. O'Neill had mixed feelings about the draw: "It was important not to get beaten but the way the game went we are all a little bit deflated in the dressing room not to have won."

SEPTEMBER 26th

Under the headline 'CLARIDGE: I'M OFF', striker Steve Claridge told the *Leicester Mercury* his City career was over. He was quoted as saying: "I feel I have gone as far as I can with Leicester and it has been great, it's been unbelievable. But I am just not happy any more. I can't see anything making a difference." Martin O'Neill revealed: "The funny thing is that since this situation came up in the papers a few days ago, I have not had one call about him."

SEPTEMBER 27th   PREM: Barnsley 0 City 2 (Marshall, Fenton)

City warmed up for the second leg of their European tie with a comfortable victory at struggling Barnsley. O'Neill: "It wasn't easy to come to Barnsley but the lads stuck to it. There is still a tremendous spirit in the dressing room."

Try as they might, nothing would fall City's way against Madrid.

Don't shoot the referee!

SEPTEMBER 30th   UEFA CUP FIRST ROUND SECOND LEG
City 0 Atletico Madrid 2 (AGG: 1-4)

One of the greatest nights in the history of Leicester City turned into a massive disappointment. The players weren't disappointing and neither were the fans. In fact, both were magnificent. But the evening was spoiled by some unbelievably strange refereeing decisions. Frenchman Remi Harrel turned a blind eye to four possible penalty decisions in City's favour, with Muzzy Izzet, involved in three of them, virtually lost for words: "I thought at least one of the penalties would have been given. I would have said three were clear." Martin O'Neill agreed with him: "I've seen the penalties on TV, I'll tell you what, they were as blatant as they come."

The referee sent off one player from each side, and infuriated City by dismissing Garry Parker for two 'bookable' offences, the second being, wait for it, taking a free kick too quickly! On top of that, Atletico grabbed two late goals to kill off the Euro dream. O'Neill described the referee as "desperately poor" (what an understatement!) and in the midst of his anger appeared to suggest that Mr Harrel might have favoured an away win. He added: "In a few days, everyone will say it was just sour grapes."

Heskey and four of the opposition (including the referee, of course!).

"Look Meester O'Neill, you give no pesetas, we give no penalties . . ."

Neil Lennon too vented his anger towards the referee: "Garry's sending off was a joke. It was THE turning point. I hate losing, especially losing the way we did." Lennon and Izzet were outstanding on the night and O'Neill described them as "world class".

A video of the match was sent to UEFA as City wanted them to judge the performance of Remi Harrel. So, a night which promised so much was ruined, in City's eyes, by one man.

OCTOBER 2nd

As he tried to put the disappointment of the Madrid game behind him, Martin O'Neill was cheered up by winning the Carling Manager of the Month award for September. His opinion of the previous match hadn't changed: "My view is still the same, even today. We can't get back into the UEFA Cup but if someone in authority can help prevent these sort of things happening again, that would be good for the game."

OCTOBER 6th   PREM: City 1 (Elliott) Derby 2

Losing to your arch rivals, live on TV as well, is just about as bad as it gets. City were made to pay for lapses in defence and Derby stole the three points, which prompted O'Neill to comment: "A quarter of the season's gone and we've done fine. But no doubt we couldn't play this level of football without adding to our squad." City were fourth.

OCTOBER 8th

Unhappy at being on the sidelines, Steve Claridge was officially put on the transfer list.

OCTOBER 10th

Relief all round as UEFA decided to take no action over Martin O'Neill's comments following the Madrid match. A spokesman said: "Mr O'Neill's explanation has been accepted and there will be no sanctions taken against him."

OCTOBER 14th   COCA-COLA CUP THIRD ROUND:
                      Grimsby 3 City 1 (Marshall)

City's defence of the Coca-Cola Cup lasted just 90 minutes in a bizarre match at Blundell Park. Cruising at 1-0 in the second half, City were well on course for victory when a series of errors let Grimsby in to snatch victory. One of these mistakes saw Kasey Keller rush out to clear the ball, but instead he punched Julian Watts, knocking him unconscious, and allowed the ball to go past him into the net. Not only that, but Steve Walsh crashed into a post trying to clear off the line. Now that's what I call a calamity! Martin O'Neill was desperately disappointed: "When they equalised we just couldn't get to grips with it. Maybe there's no Europe at the end of it but I wanted to get back to Wembley and I thought the players wanted that too."

OCTOBER 16th

UEFA announced that Remi Harrel, the man in charge of City's cup-tie with Madrid, would not officiate in any more games in this season's competition. At least Europe's governing body seemed to agree with O'Neill's post match analysis of the Frenchman.

OCTOBER 18th   PREM: Chelsea 1 City 0

One Frenchman that O'Neill couldn't criticise was his own goalkeeper Pegguy Arphexad. Kasey Keller's understudy made his debut at Stamford Bridge, as the American was injured, and he made some breathtaking saves. The only one he couldn't keep out was a 35-yard shot in the dying seconds . . . hit by another

Frenchman, Frank Leboeuf. City's patched-up team were praised by O'Neill who said: "I thought the players did fantastically well in the circumstances. I could not have asked for more from them." City were now fifth.

OCTOBER 23rd
Bryan Hamilton's sacking as manager of the Northern Ireland national team prompted speculation linking O'Neill with the job, either on a part-time or full-time basis.

OCTOBER 24th
A momentous day in the history of Leicester City as the club was floated on the stock market, at a value of £36 million. However, share prices soon fell dramatically and carried on dropping over the following few weeks. By February 1998, the price was under 50p per share, less than half the original price.

OCTOBER 27th   PREM: City 2 (Heskey, Marshall) West Ham United 1
Ian Marshall's late winner came as a huge relief to the City boss as he was getting a little edgy on the sidelines. "If we had lost this that would have been five on the trot," he said, "and we all would have been getting anxious, but the pressure is slightly off." City returned to fourth place and Marshall was delighted to get the all-important goal: "After four defeats, people were starting to ask questions, so it was great to get a result."

LATE OCTOBER
Injured keeper Kasey Keller, who had kept six clean sheets in nine World Cup qualifiers, was named USA Footballer of the Year. And summer signing Graham Fenton dismissed talk that he was unsettled at Filbert Street. Fenton, a regular on the substitutes bench, said it was "nonsense" to suggest he was unhappy.

Heskey's horror

NOVEMBER 1st   PREM: Newcastle 3 City 3 (Marshall 2, Elliott)
What do City have to do to get a win at St James's Park? Last time they squandered a 3-1 lead to lose; on this occasion they were twice ahead and ended up conceding an injury time equaliser. That disappointment became worse when Emile Heskey was sent off for tussling with Phillipe Albert. Heskey said: "I retaliated with him and was sent off. But I pushed him, not punched him. I would like a bit more protection from referees."

NOVEMBER 3rd
Record signing Matt Elliott was called into the Scotland squad for the friendly with France. Elliott, dubbed MacElliott by team-mates, was born in Surrey, but qualified

Thanks to his late grandmother. He said: "It's a great honour to be picked for the national squad. I have got a lot of relatives that still live up in Scotland and they will be delighted. The last 10 months have been an amazing sequence of events."

NOVEMBER 9th
City were linked with Manchester City's Georgian superstar Georgi Kinkladze in a Sunday newspaper. They quoted the price as £5 million but Martin O'Neill said: "It's absolute rubbish."

NOVEMBER 10th   PREM: City 0 Wimbledon 1
City were really off colour in a dreadful match, again in front of Sky TV. Neil Lennon pulled no punches: "We played badly in a game we should have won because we fell short of having the right attitude. We can't afford to drop our standards. It might just be the lesson we need."

NOVEMBER 12th
City's handling of the travel arrangements for the UEFA Cup match in Spain came in for stern criticism in an independent report. The study said: "Fans were 'justifiably dissatisfied' with many aspects." City's reaction came from Tom Smeaton, who claimed: "We cannot be held solely responsible." Some supporters decided to pursue legal action.

Meanwhile, Matt Elliott made his Scotland debut in France, coming on as a second half substitute. And striker Tony Cottee was allowed to go on loan to First Division Birmingham.

Sinclair £5m tag

Huge fee could
force O'Neill
out of market

NOVEMBER 17th
The newspapers were getting desperate for Martin O'Neill to spend his money. First it was Kinkladze, now it was the turn of Queens Park Rangers winger Trevor Sinclair to be linked with a big money move to Filbert Street. Again, the price tag was said to be £5 million, surely out of City's price range? O'Neill announced that he wasn't going to sign players just for the sake of it: "The quality players I want to bring to the club are just not available at the moment."

NOVEMBER 22nd   PREM: City 0 Bolton 0
Another disappointing home display from City. They just couldn't get the ball in the back of the net with Marshall and Izzet both among the guilty men missing chances. City, without the suspended Heskey, now found themselves seventh, below rivals Derby.

NOVEMBER 29th   PREM: Coventry 0 City 2 (Fenton, Elliott)

City's first win at Highfield Road in 21 years came courtesy of a goal in each half and a display which bore all the hallmarks of O'Neill's time at Filbert Street. It was a gutsy, determined performance in horrible wet and muddy conditions and took them three points nearer to 42, the target set by O'Neill to avoid relegation. But Neil Lennon was more optimistic, keeping an eye on the European places: "We are not the Manchester Uniteds of this world, we haven't got their strength in depth. We definitely have got a chance of qualifying for Europe."

O'Neill was asked in the press conference who he hoped to sign to strengthen his depleted squad. He replied: "The players are holding the fort until we get a couple of Del Pieros!"

IZZET IZ THE BIZ Muzzy rescues O'Neill crocks

DECEMBER 6th   PREM: City 1 (Izzet) Crystal Palace 1

He doesn't score many, but when they do go in, they're normally a bit special. Muzzy Izzet's 90th minute goal was a beauty and rescued a point for injury-hit City who had been frustrated all afternoon by 10-man Palace. Steve Coppell, the Palace boss, said: "He did a Tom Finney to curl the ball over our goalkeeper and into the top corner." O'Neill again bemoaned their lack of strength in depth: "We even had to pull a lad out of the youth team to make up the numbers on the bench. But I have to be happy with a point that keeps us in the top six." Ian Marshall was missing from the City line-up due to a groin injury which needed an operation.

DECEMBER 8th

Martin O'Neill stunned listeners to Radio Leicester's phone-in when he made a call to the programme totally out of the blue. O'Neill had been driving along when one particular caller really riled the City boss. O'Neill blew his top when the man described his efforts to buy players as going at 'a snails pace'.

He stormed: "He is the egghead of eggheads where football is concerned. This is the man who called Simon Grayson and Mike Whitlow 'cloggers' 18 or 20 months ago. We sold them for £2 million. He also said, after five weeks in the job, that I'd had enough time to sort things out. Look how things have turned round. And now he's saying we should push for a European place. How delightful. We are up there in the Premiership and it isn't a fluke."

O'Neill continued his tirade: "I have never actually PROMISED a signing but I'm always trying to strengthen the squad. There is no-one more anxious than me to get quality players in. But we need to make sure we get value for money. Eighteen months ago, I had to do two things. One, I had to sell before I could buy, and two, I had to be successful. I was criticised for selling Steve Corica for £1.5 million and getting Neil Lennon in for £750,000. The same caller - that egghead - actually criticised that deal.

What a year! Lennon and Walsh celebrate THE night of the past 12 months.

"When we signed Muzzy Izzet, it was 'Muzzy who?' from the fans. Now you would have to say he's probably worth £4 million. As for new signings, the players I want are not always available for a variety of reasons. I could have sold Graham Fenton and got my money back twice on him in recent weeks, but I've refused to do so."

O'Neill was asked by the programme's frontman, highly respected Midlands journalist Neville Foulger, about signing foreign players. He said: "We are not in the league to sign the likes of Zola and Juninho much as we'd like to. Take Zola, a choice between London giants Chelsea and Leicester City where we were just over a year ago, I think he wouldn't have had a problem making that decision."

He ended by outlining his determination to carry on delivering the goods at Filbert Street: "I want to take Leicester as far as I can."

Bill Anderson, in his *Leicester Mercury* column, hit the nail on the head. He wrote: "If his reaction to that phone call is anything to go by, if this sort of carping goes on, even if it does in fact reflect a minuscule minority, that might still not be enough for O'Neill, who has not forgotten the disgraceful barracking of two seasons ago, to feel like picking up the phone again. This time, though, the call could be to one of several clubs already eyeing his talents."

DECEMBER 9th
Speculation linked City with a move away from Filbert Street to a purpose-built brand new stadium.

DECEMBER 13th   PREM: Southampton 2 City 1 (Savage)
A stunning late goal from Robbie Savage was not enough to rescue a point for City in a game they perhaps should have won. Again, Kasey Keller was lucky to stay on the field for a foul outside the box and Martin O'Neill said: "You could say we were a bit fortunate but it is a bit of a grey area."

Goalscorer Savage staked his claim for a regular place but was disappointed with the eventual result: "While I am delighted to have scored my first goal for City, we lost which is the most important thing. I know I can score goals from midfield and I'll get my share if I get a run in the side."

DECEMBER 17th
Emile Heskey helped himself to two goals in England's 4-2 victory over Greece in the Under 21 Championships but the national team bowed out on the away goals rule.

I AM SO LUCKY TO BE ALIVE!

DECEMBER 18th

City defender Spencer Prior was an injury concern for Saturday's match with Everton after a nasty car accident. Prior crashed his BMW into a tree at 50mph but managed to escape with just whiplash and a cut face. He said: "I'm lucky to be alive, the airbag saved my life. If it hadn't been such a strong car, it might have been a different story."

DECEMBER 20th   PREM: City 0 Everton 1

City's home jinx rumbled on as Everton snatched victory with a last minute penalty which Martin O'Neill, wrongly in my opinion, strongly criticised. Of referee Jeff Winter, he commented: "It was not one of his better days. I have to say some of his decisions were baffling."

After 19 games of the campaign, City had 27 points and were still in eighth place. O'Neill's reaction was: "If you'd said to me at the start of the season that at the halfway point we would be one place ahead of the likes of Newcastle and in a higher position than we finished last season, then we would have taken it. It could have been better of course. Today showed again that we are not taking our chances to make our superiority count."

DECEMBER 26th   PREM: Arsenal 2 City 1 (Lennon)

A bizarre own goal from Steve Walsh proved to be too much for City whose comeback couldn't quite match the one which rescued them against Arsenal earlier in the season. Neil Lennon's late goal gave them hope but Arsene Wenger's title challengers hung on. O'Neill said: "I thought this was the right time to play Arsenal. I told the players that before the match, and again at half time, that we had a chance here. But we had a lack of passion and we base our game on that. We put in a grandstand finish but it just wasn't good enough."

DECEMBER 28th   PREM: City 1 (Guppy) Sheffield Wednesday 1

Andy Booth made sure it was an unhappy Christmas for City with a late equaliser at Filbert Street. If it had been a boxing match, it would have been stopped long before that as City were well ahead on the proverbial points. They were a goal up thanks to a rare first half Guppy header, but after Wednesday had a man sent off they squandered chance after chance, and let Ron Atkinson's team back in. Steve Claridge thought he'd won it for City in injury time but the substitute had a goal disallowed (harshly, it seemed) for pushing.

In the post-match press conference, O'Neill said: "I'm heartily sick because that's the best we have played since beating Tottenham in September. To be pegged back like that feels as bad as a defeat. We could have won this game 12-2 or 12-3 and I mean that. It's been a fantastic year but we just couldn't manage to end it in style."

City ended 1997 in ninth place, a fantastic achievement. But amazingly, it could have been even better had they picked up more than just 10 points out of a possible 36 in the last 12 games of the year. They entered 1998 determined to get back to winning ways and so it proved. With O'Neill at the helm, everything seems possible!

SCARING THE OPPOSITION

ESSENTIAL BEDTIME READING FOR THE LEICESTER CITY BOSS

SCARY HESKEY   GINGER LENNON   POSH MUZZY   BABY SAVAGE   SPORTY GUPPY

ARE THE LEICESTER CITY SPICE BOYS!

HILLSBOROUGH
APRIL 16TH 1997
CLARIDGE FIRES
THE FOXES INTO
EUROPE!

PART TWO

MARTIN O'NEILL – THE STATISTICS
21st December 1995 - 28th December 1997

ALL COMPETITIONS (HOME & AWAY)
PLAYED 104
WON 38
DRAWN 38
LOST 34
GOALS FOR 123
GOALS AGAINST 123

(HOME) **ALL COMPETITIONS** (AWAY)
52 PLAYED 52
19 WON 19
19 DRAWN 13
14 LOST 20
59 GOALS FOR 64
54 GOALS AGAINST 69

PREMIERSHIP (HOME & AWAY)
PLAYED 59
WON 19
DRAWN 18
LOST 22
GOALS FOR 71
GOALS AGAINST 75

(HOME) **PREMIERSHIP** (AWAY)
31 PLAYED 28
10 WON 9
11 DRAWN 7
10 LOST 12
35 GOALS FOR 36
37 GOALS AGAINST 38

CUP COMPETITIONS (HOME & AWAY)
PLAYED 18
WON 8
DRAWN 5
LOST 5
GOALS FOR 20
GOALS AGAINST 19

(HOME) **CUP COMPETITIONS** (AWAY)
8 PLAYED 10
4 WON 4
3 DRAWN 2
1 LOST 4
10 GOALS FOR 10
6 GOALS AGAINST 13

DIVISION ONE (HOME & AWAY)PLAYED 24
WON 9
DRAWN 8
LOST 7
GOALS FOR 29
GOALS AGAINST 28

(HOME) **DIVISION ONE** (AWAY)
12 PLAYED 12
5 WON 4
4 DRAWN 4
3 LOST 4
14 GOALS FOR 15
11 GOALS AGAINST 17

PLAY OFF GAMES (HOME & AWAY)
PLAYED 3
WON 2
DRAWN 1
LOST 0.
GOALS FOR 3
GOALS AGAINST 1

BIGGEST WIN (Division One) 3-0 v Birmingham (home)
BIGGEST WIN (Premiership) 4-2 v Derby (home) Blackburn (away)
BIGGEST WIN (Cup) 2-0 v Scarborough (away) York (away) Man Utd (home)
Southend (home)
BIGGEST DEFEAT (Division One) 4-2 v Ipswich (away)
BIGGEST DEFEAT (Premiership) 3-0 v Liverpool (home)
BIGGEST DEFEAT (Cup) 5-0 v Manchester City (away)

FACTS:

Martin O'Neill's first 104 matches are equally split with 52 home and 52 away.
Their 38 wins are also equally split with 19 home and 19 away.
They have scored the same number of goals as they've conceded (123).
City have scored more goals away (64) than at home (59).
They have also conceded more away (69) than at home (54).
City have been unbeaten in 70 of their 104 games.
City have kept 33 clean sheets in 104 games.
Of their 38 wins, 23 were by a single goal, the other 15 by two or more.
Of their 34 defeats, 18 were by a single goal, the other 16 by two or more.
City's biggest defeat in any competition was 5-0 at Manchester City in the FA Cup.
City's biggest win (by margin) was 3-0 v Birmingham City.
City's biggest wins (highest score) were 4-2 v Derby and Blackburn.
City have conceded four goals in a Premiership match once, v Newcastle 4-3.
Martin O'Neill really, really loves statistics (!)
These statistics are correct up to 28/12/97.

BOUGHT AND SOLD BY MARTIN O'NEILL

December 1995 - December 1997

SIGNED BY O'NEILL . . . . **SOLD BY O'NEILL**

Neil Lennon £750,00 . . . . Steve Corica £1,500,000
Steve Claridge £1,200,000 . . . . Julian Joachim £1,500,000
Julian Watts £210,000 . . . . Simon Grayson £1,350,000
Muzzy Izzet £650,000 . . . . Iwan Roberts £1,250,000
Spencer Prior £600,000 . . . . Mike Whitlow £750,000
Kasey Keller £900,000 . . . . Neil Lewis £60,000
Ian Marshall £925,000 . . . . Jamie Lawrence £50,000
Matt Elliott £1,600,000 . . . . Brian Carey £50,000
Rob Ullathorne £600,000 . . . . David Lowe £50,000
Steve Guppy £850,000 . . . . Richard Smith £50,000
Rob Savage £400,000 . . . . A number of other
Pegguy Arphexad free . . . . players left
Graham Fenton £1,100,000 . . . . the club on
Tony Cottee £500,000 . . . . free transfers

TOTALS:

£10,285,000 SPENT . . . . **RECEIVED £6,560,000**

A DEFICIT OF £3,725,000.

A storm developed in February 1998 over the amount of money that Martin O'Neill has spent since he took over as manager. In a letter to the *Leicester Mercury*, City chairman Tom Smeaton said O'Neill's net spending was £5.6 million, which included the signing in January of Theo Zagorakis from Greek side PAOK Salonika, which isn't included in the above figures.

O'Neill hit back at Smeaton's claims and said: "Actually he must have sneaked a player or two in that which I haven't discovered yet! Before I signed Theo Zagorakis, I reckon I was just below £4 million in transfers - and he was only £750,000 - so I don't know where Mr Smeaton gets that £5.6 million from."

The City boss added: "When I came into the club in December 1995, I was given one instruction - to win promotion. There was no money around but any money generated in the transfer market could be used for extra players, which I was happy enough to go along with. A couple of players left, like Steve Corica, David Lowe and Julian Joachim, and in came Claridge, Lennon and Watts and initially Muzzy Izzet on loan, so by June 1996 we had got promotion and I was £1 million to the good.

"We had a situation the following year when we were in the Premiership and we knew there would be Sky money floating around," he told the *Leicester Mercury*. "We then allowed Iwan Roberts to leave and were able to buy Keller and Prior. Later on, in September, Ian Marshall arrived and Izzet was signed for £650,000. I was out about £1 million at that time.

"Matt Elliott was bought in January of last year - we ended up winning the Coca-Cola Cup, finishing ninth in the Premiership and all, by my reckoning, on a deficit of £3 million."

O'Neill, angry about his chairman's comments, finished by saying: "We have established ourselves in the Premiership and won the Coca Cola Cup to qualify for Europe in my time here and it has been done for about £1.2 million a year."

SOME MIGHT SAY

EARLY 1998: After a disappointing end to the previous 12 months, which was a fantastic year by Leicester City's standards, 1998 began with a bang. A win against Manchester United at Old Trafford, plus home victories over Leeds and Chelsea, and draws against Liverpool, Spurs and Villa rekindled City's hopes of a European place for a second year running. Again, the team proved that they tend to raise their game against the big boys. When the going gets tough, as they say, City become giants. The only black spots in the early part of the year came away from home, losing 3-0 at Crystal Palace in the FA Cup, 5-3 at Blackburn in an astonishing match and 2-1 at struggling Wimbledon. During the good run of results, seven unbeaten in the League in fact, we reflected on the first two years of Martin O'Neill's reign with a number of players, ex-players, journalists and one or two other interested observers. Here's what they had to say.

PRE-MARTIN O'NEILL

STEVE WALSH, who has played under numerous bosses at Leicester since 1986: "I wouldn't say we were down at this point, it was just a matter of waiting to see what was going to happen, and who was going to be appointed. As players, you've just got to get on with it, the same when any manager goes."

SIMON GRAYSON, who joined City in 1992 and was a first team regular under O'Neill: "Obviously with it being the second time in about a year we were all a bit unsure about what was going to happen. Everybody was a little uncertain about their futures, whoever was to come in and take over, whether it be Martin O'Neill, Mike Walker or someone else."

BILL ANDERSON, chief soccer writer for the Leicester Mercury: "Everyone says he wasn't City's first choice but I don't think they had decided for definite who they wanted. It's true to say that the majority of the Board wanted Mike Walker, even when it emerged that Martin O'Neill had left Norwich. Martin George and Robert Chase (the Norwich chairman) were discussing another matter when George asked Chase which of the two men he would recommend. Now, it was in Robert Chase's interests to say Walker, for various reasons, but he said O'Neill, by a long way. This made an impression on Martin George which he conveyed to the rest of the Board. They weren't necessarily convinced. Since, obviously, he's been proved right, and the others, many of whom are still there, were wrong."

One word to sum up Martin O'Neill – passion.

MARTIN O'NEILL'S ARRIVAL

PONTUS KAAMARK, signed by Mark McGhee: "There was a lot of turbulence. We didn't know what to expect at first when he arrived so it can't have been easy for him either. It was the middle of the season, there were players he didn't know much about and vice versa, but we were lucky to come through, eventually, with the trip to Wembley."

STEVE WALSH, signed by Bryan Hamilton: "It was a difficult start. But I think it will always be like that because you're getting to know people. We were adjusting to his ways which we did find difficult at first, and that did cause problems. He soon rectified those.

"I think the problems off the field could have caused our poor results on it. But then again we didn't have the right personnel either which we knew. We had a great start to that season but we were struggling when Mark McGhee left, even though we were there or thereabouts near the top. If I remember rightly we had lost a few games under him and we were on a bit of a slump at the time. We slumped even further after that."

BILL ANDERSON: "Certain people upstairs were quite happy to see Martin O'Neill fall flat on his face. My sympathy lies entirely with him coming into that situation. They (on the Board) would have seen it as a personal reflection on Martin George, who stuck his neck out for O'Neill, if the manager had failed."

SIMON GRAYSON, signed by Brian Little: "When a new manager comes in, he's got to get that respect off the players and put his own authority down. The previous manager had gone about it in a different way, but everybody has their own methods.

"Looking back, it was a difficult time at first, but I wouldn't say that the off field problems affected us in games. Despite all that, he's gone on to have a lot of success."

O'NEILL'S FIRST WIN – AT MARK McGHEE'S WOLVES

STEVE WALSH: "We won 3-2 and with what had happened it was a big night for us. All that mattered was that we were playing Mark McGhee, who was manager there and we wanted to put one over him. We wanted to show him what he'd left behind. And it was a bit of a turning point, yeah. Although the main turning point had to be the Sheffield United game."

SIMON GRAYSON: "A turning point, definitely. At that stage of the season you have to start winning games if you're going to be in contention for the play-offs. It was always going to be a highly charged game with what had happened. Everybody was fired up, the players, the staff and the fans, and as it turned out we got the win. Victory was definitely that little bit sweeter with it being against our ex-manager."

THE SALE OF JULIAN JOACHIM

STEVE WALSH, who played up front with Joachim for part of the 92-93 season: "He had a foot injury which upset his rhythm, he had an operation and he came back not quite as we expected. He couldn't find a level of consistency, due to the injury, which you need over a full season. Then he got a good move to Aston Villa. I still rate him, he's still learning, but you have to remember he's still young and that's a key factor. He's been in and out of the Villa side but he's done alright recently. He scored against us of course in January and he's been looking like he might get back to his old form. Julian's a useful player no doubt about that. Martin obviously thought the time was probably right to sell him."

PLAYERS SIGNED BY O'NEILL – WHY JOIN CITY?

NEIL LENNON, a bargain at £750,000: "I didn't know anything about the club really when I first came down and I didn't know anything about the city. I was supposed to go to Coventry and it was a gamble going to a Division One club but the gaffer came and spoke to me and he convinced me to sign. He and John Robertson (O'Neill's assistant) were the two main reasons why I came."

KASEY KELLER, who joined City in the summer of 1996 from Millwall: "Martin O'Neill was very persuasive. I had a year left on my contract at Millwall, they'd just been relegated and they needed the money. I nearly went to Germany but the money wasn't right for Millwall and then a call came out of the blue from City. Everyone was saying that Leicester would be relegated by Christmas and, looking at it from a pessimistic view, I had to weigh up whether one year in the Premier League was worth it, when I could stay at Millwall for 12 months and get a free transfer. I decided, obviously, to take the chance."

MATT ELLIOTT, who signed from Oxford for a club record £1.6 million in January 1997: "I didn't know that much about his style of management. It was a late night/early morning meeting when we got together and he brought his coaching staff as well as the chairman. I was impressed that he deemed it important enough to bring them along. His enthusiasm shone through at that stage. I was surprised by how much he really wanted to sign me and I took that as a big compliment."

ROBBIE SAVAGE, who followed Neil Lennon from Crewe to Leicester: "First of all I spoke to John Robertson, the assistant manager, and he impressed me, especially with his stature in the game. Then the gaffer called me from where he was on holiday and he seemed keen. He said: 'If I get to like you, I'll always like you' so I knew where I stood. He's the fairest manager I've known. I think he's one of the best in the league, and I'm not just saying that because he's the gaffer. His enthusiasm stands out. He's like me - always giving 100%. He gets so excited, I think he's wonderful."

GARRY PARKER STRIPPED OF THE CAPTAINCY. A STORM IN A TEACUP?

STEVE WALSH: "It was blown out of all proportion. It was a thing that goes on in dressing rooms and that was a dressing room incident that should be kept there. We've had two or three more with myself and other players but you just get on with things. I've had my own personal things with Martin O'Neill but that's just a reaction after a game if something's happened and then it's forgotten, as it should be. You need to talk about things, get them into the open, then apologise and that's it; end of story.

PONTUS KAAMARK, who's now very careful when he speaks to journalists: "I wasn't playing at the time but I heard from the others that him (O'Neill) and Parks threw water over each other at half time because there were disagreements. That just shows how serious and important things are, with their passion coming through. Obviously they weren't physically fighting but if things don't go right, and people want to win so much, these things can happen. We all give each other stick but it shows the team spirit."

SIMON GRAYSON: "I think it was slightly over-exaggerated in the press. These things happen week in and week out at all clubs and at the time we were going through a tricky period. Obviously Garry lost the captaincy after it, but it does prove that he (O'Neill) doesn't bear grudges because he (Parker) is still there now. It was an argument out of nothing really, I don't even know what it was about, things got heated and they both showed the passion of wanting to be successful."

STEVE WALSH: "I suppose it does show passion on his (O'Neill) and my part. He does get very irate at times but it's only because of the passion, you can see that. I think early on we found it hard to deal with. Even this season, two or three of us have had really horrible things that happened in the dressing room, but it's gone now. I can't say too much obviously."

HOME TO SHEFFIELD UNITED – AND <u>THAT</u> DEFEAT

NEIL LENNON: "This was definitely the turning point as far as I was concerned. I was suspended after getting sent off at Oldham the week before and Muzzy and Julian Watts made their debut. We were terrible, really awful. We got what we deserved - a 2-0 defeat. I think things were coming to a head with the fans, there was a demonstration and all that. I'm glad I wasn't playing but I felt really sorry for the lads that did because they got severe stick. The gaffer got loads of stick."

MUZZY IZZET, another of O'Neill's excellent value for money signings: "Things weren't going too well and I remember Martin O'Neill putting me on in the closing stages. I enjoyed it - making my debut - but it was probably the low point in terms of result and overall performance. The crowd got on top of O'Neill and didn't really give him a chance."

STEVE WALSH: "Wolves was a bit of a turning point but this definitely was. We were shocking that day. But we went on from there, we beat Palace and Charlton away from home, they were two really important games. It was a backs against the wall job in those two wins and things went on from there."

SIMON GRAYSON: "It was pretty much the worst performance that season. There was a lot of stick flying around at the players and the management, and that was another turning point. We talked about it and used it as an inspiration for it to never happen again and take strength from it. We desperately wanted to prove everybody wrong."

DAVID NEILSON, aka Coronation Street's cafe owner Roy Cropper. A big City fan: "We have followed so many false messiahs in the past who were going to do big things that we've learned to expect the worst. When everything happened during the Sheffield United game, you could sort of understand why the fans did what they did, but unfortunately they were venting their frustration at the wrong man. He was actually on the verge of turning it all around."

BILL ANDERSON: "The reaction of the fans was a disgrace, it was ridiculous. There were hundreds of them shouting 'f*** off' O'Neill and then turning around and saying it was aimed at the Board. Martin O'Neill's response to that was: 'Which director is called O'Neill?' There is no excuse for that. And he will never forget that. When they went through the pantomime of inviting some fans in to meet Tom Smeaton what they should have done, in hindsight, was take the names and addresses and make sure they never got Wembley tickets for either the play-offs or the Coca-Cola Cup. I agree they weren't the majority, but they were a sizeable vocal minority.

"In many ways, that hardened his resolve to be a success. He said to the players: 'I'm not going to let this beat me' and he was right."

NEIL LENNON: "The gaffer got us in on the Monday and I swear to God, this is what he said. He goes: 'I'll take all the stick now, you lot get me to Wembley and win promotion, and I'll take all the plaudits then' and he was true to his word. It must have been a terrible time for him because he did come under a lot of personal abuse, which was, at the time, uncalled for. He'd only been in the job for two or three months! You can see why the fans were like that but I hadn't been at the club long enough to appreciate what had gone on before (Little & McGhee walking out), and how the fans really felt. I thought 'What have I done?' but it soon worked out for us."

END OF THE LEAGUE SEASON 1996

MUZZY IZZET: "Even though the Sheffield United match was dire, I didn't think I'd made a mistake in joining Leicester. I was pleased to be playing first team football. We just got better and better with each game towards the end of the season, playing good football. Then we went to Watford, and I scored the winner, and that got us in the play-offs."

NEIL LENNON: "Steve Claridge scored his first goal for us a few days after the Sheffield United game at Charlton and we won one-nil and things just turned round. Then we beat Palace, lost to West Brom, drew at Tranmere and then won four on the trot to get in the play-offs."

SIMON GRAYSON: "I remember we'd just signed Steve Claridge for a million or so and he scored some vital goals. That's what you need to do, go on a good run, and we won six of our last eight matches."

DAVID NEILSON: "The whole run-in was amazing. Once they beat Watford to get into the play offs, I just knew they were going to go all the way. It was just the whole momentum thing, winning six games after the Sheffield United debacle."

FIRST DIVISION PLAY-OFFS

PONTUS KAAMARK: "I was injured and missed out. Obviously you want to be playing every game especially good moments like beating Palace at Wembley. I just wanted to be on the pitch. I was delighted to come to a club who went up straight away even though I didn't do much to help them into the Premiership of course. I signed for a First Division club and when I started my career properly here, we were in the Premiership."

NEIL LENNON: "The first leg was terrible. The pitch at Filbert Street was a mess and really and truly we should have been two goals down but Kevin Poole kept us in it. Then the second leg was on a much better pitch at Stoke. Parks scored an absolute pearler and that was that."

MUZZY IZZET: "I remember getting a lucky draw at home and then winning away. We played ever so well in the second leg."

SIMON GRAYSON, one of City's play-off veterans: "We could have been dead and buried after the first leg but Pooley made some fantastic saves. Everybody wrote us off after that saying we'd blown our chance, and that's the mistake everyone makes. You should never write Leicester off. We went out and proved people wrong in the second leg to get to Wembley again."

STEVE WALSH: "We played Stoke, it was a tricky tie. We were still confident even after we drew the home leg and I think we handled it very well. We were a strong unit on the night, in the second leg, and deserved to go through."

NEIL LENNON: "There was me, Larry (Simon Grayson) and Muzzy who came off the pitch in just our underwear! There was a pitch invasion by Stoke fans and we had to get police protection behind the goal for about 20 minutes until they got them all off. I threw my jersey into the crowd but people were grabbing shorts and stuff and I was lucky to get back to the changing room with my boots!"

Post-Wembley '96 – We all stand together: the unbelievable team spirit.

STEVE WALSH, two-goal Wembley hero against Derby in 1994: "As for the final, it was superb for me, absolutely. The win enabled us to compete with the best again. Under Martin we have created a team that goes down for me as one of the best I've played in without a doubt. In fact, it's THE best. I suppose I've got to thank him for the good times, like this win, which I've had since he's been here. To captain the side and actually win was amazing. I didn't want to go there as captain and lose because I did that obviously against Blackburn in 1992. I lost my captaincy to Gary Mills the next year, then Simon Grayson was skipper when we won in '94. I would have loved to have been captain for that one, but I suppose scoring the winner made up for that!"

MUZZY IZZET: "To play at Wembley was a dream come true, and to win there was fantastic, just brilliant. The manager didn't need to fire us up, he did say a few things but it's all about self-motivation. It happened so quick from playing in Chelsea reserves to playing at Wembley in a short space of time."

NEVILLE FOULGER, Veteran journalist and BBC Radio Leicester's best commentator: "It's difficult to find the right words to describe the play-off final. I suppose it was bizarre in many ways. Everybody was preparing for a penalty shoot-out; the players, the management, us in the commentary box. Martin O'Neill had sent on Zeljko Kalac in the last minute of extra time and probably felt that Zeljko, at six foot seven, would perhaps help in terms of putting off the Palace players in a penalty shoot-out. Everyone was looking at Kalac when the free kick was lumped forward and it just fell to Steve Claridge, who later said he hardly had any energy left. Then he swung a boot at it and time stood still. It seemed to float in in slow motion. It was the most unexpected goal I think I've ever seen."

SIMON GRAYSON, Wembley captain in 1994: "The emotions were so high, it was unbelievable. One-nil down with time running out, you start to wonder. But we managed to equalise and that lifted us. Then scoring with effectively the last kick of the season was a thrill and a buzz that you can't really describe. Time just seemed to stop still, Claridge just hit it and there it was, in the back of the net. At that time of the game you know you're not going to lose."

BILL ANDERSON: "I was sitting in the press box waiting for the end of extra time and penalties when I turned to my colleague Graham Melton, who was writing something, and I said: 'Claridge'. He looked up just as the ball hit the back of the net. There was a deathly hush for a second or so and that was it. There's been plenty of dramatic finishes in recent years, especially at Wembley, and it was only really 24 hours later when it had all been done and dusted that it sunk in. I'm not a City fan, but it was really good."

PETER JONES, Loughborough-based Premiership referee and big City fan: "I was one of two England FA representatives refereeing at the Toulon tournament in the south of France. It just happened that the day of the play-off final, I was refereeing Argentina against Russia, and I was really desperate to find out how City were getting on. So I borrowed someone's mobile phone before the match and I called a friend of mine in Leicester. He said it was perfect timing because Steve Claridge had just scored the winner. It was fantastic."

DAVID NEILSON, who couldn't persuade Coronation Street bosses to adjust their filming schedule to allow him to go to Wembley: "I managed to see extra time on TV in Manchester where we were filming but before that I listened to it on a walkman. It was one of the most disappointing things in my life that I wasn't there. We were on location that day and it was at the point where I was still freaking Deirdre out in the show. We were in the flat filming and I remember us getting the penalty just before we were about to shoot a scene. There was no way I could film anything until after the penalty! So everyone had to stop while I listened to it on headphones. We scored, we finished the scene and off I went to find a TV to watch the drama unfold. To be Steve Claridge to score that goal must be the best feeling ever in the world. Fantastic."

NEIL LENNON: "The final, for me, was like the highlight of the two years, no doubt about it. It was just our day, better even than the Coca-Cola Cup win. It was amazing because Claridge hit it with his shin or something and it just went straight in, in slow motion. There's a photograph of Claridge running away with his hands on his head, a face looking in disbelief, and me and Muzzy in the background, and I've got a big smile on my face. That just encapsulated the whole thing for me. It's so hard to describe how you felt."

CITY'S GREAT RUN OF RESULTS AGAINST ASTON VILLA

STEVE WALSH, who speaks as highly of Brian Little as Little does of him: "We've done well, yeah. I don't think we're extra fired up as it is, or was Brian Little as manager before he resigned, it's just another game for us. That vendetta went out of the window a long time ago. It's always important when you play Aston Villa, like anyone in the Premiership, to do well. They're a big club but we're as good as them, simple as that."

NEIL LENNON: "People have tagged us that we always do well against the bigger clubs and I suppose to a certain extent that's true."

SIMON GRAYSON, sold to Villa in the summer of 1997 for £1.35 million: "I've been on both sides . . . winning against Villa and Brian Little, and being at Villa when Leicester beat us. Obviously the first few games when Brian had left Leicester were a bit special because it was really hyped up. You always want to do well against your former club or former manager. There just seems to be this hoodoo Leicester have over Villa. I remember once being 4-1 down at Villa with a few minutes left and drawing 4-4, that's the kind of thing that can happen. Since Martin took over, Leicester's good run has continued. They beat us in the first game of this season, and then we drew at Villa Park. It's just one of those things that's hard to explain."

DIVISION ONE TO THE PREMIERSHIP – THE TRANSFORMATION

MUZZY IZZET, from Chelsea reserve to top flight regular: "It was hard because you're coming up against better players in better teams and that's bound to be tough. After about 10/12 games, you start getting the hang of it, you start realising you've got a little bit more time as the players sit off you a bit. In the First Division, it's all crash-bang-wallop, kick-b*****k-goodbye."

SIMON GRAYSON, who played in City's forgettable 94-95 Premiership campaign: "I think we were better prepared this time round. Everybody wrote us off, and said we'd go straight back down, but we prepared differently and had a couple of new signings to strengthen the squad which was important. Getting off to a good start was a major thing and we had four points after two games, which lifted confidence."

KASEY KELLER: "We drew the first game, won the second and that was a big improvement from two years before. I think it took something like five or six games to get the first point then, so that made a big difference. Also, we kept a clean sheet in the first game, whereas the previous time it took them until about November! It gave us a big boost to get off on the right foot."

NEVILLE FOULGER, who has reported Leicester City since 1987: "I think the squad was better than the first time they went up under Brian Little. Martin had already made one or two signings and you have to say they were good ones, like those that followed. More came and they gelled so well. That was the key."

DECEMBER 1996 – O'NEILL LINKED WITH NOTTINGHAM FOREST

STEVE WALSH: "When this kind of thing happens, or speculation that it might happen, we just have to get on with it. You just never know what's going to happen. You don't turn a blind eye to it going on around you, we knew what was going on and I suppose it was a possibility. He's got his own little goals and aims and who knows when he's going to go. The way he is managing at the moment, the way the team is going, I can't see them holding on to him a lot longer.

"He's ambitious but we don't know what he's thinking or what he wants to do exactly. I know he wants to take us as far as he can although we don't know how much further he can take us. I suppose it's how much money he is given. He needs the backing. He's proved his worth, bought very good players, and made us into a strong force."

KASEY KELLER: "As a player, you know that managers come and go and you can't do a lot about it. It was in the backs of our minds but it's out of our control."

NEIL LENNON: "I don't think there was any danger that the gaffer would leave anyway. John Robertson is the one who always comes in and reassures you and he said there's no way Martin is going. He was offered the job when he was at Wycombe but he turned it down then. I think the fans were more sceptical about it than we were."

BILL ANDERSON: "It was always unlikely, in my opinion, that he would go to Forest then. I used to joke with him that I wouldn't be sending him a Christmas card because he'd be gone by then, like Little and McGhee.

"I think the public drew the wrong parallel between Brian Little and Aston Villa, and Martin O'Neill and Nottingham Forest. Little had Villa blood in his veins. Martin did not think the same way about Forest. Allan Evans said in November 1994 that if it was any other club than Villa, then Brian would have stayed. I can assure you that neither John Robertson or Martin O'Neill have that same feeling that Forest is the be all and end all."

JANUARY 1997 – DEFEAT AT LEEDS – CITY 5TH BOTTOM

PONTUS KAAMARK: "It wasn't really panic at that point but we weren't playing well then. Obviously you start looking below you at the relegation places but you really have to take the games one at a time. We know results and performances can go up and down and we know we have to battle hard for every point. Things were starting to get a little bit scary, but we got through it."

NEIL LENNON: "It was one of the worst performances of the season. Thankfully I didn't play in it!"

SIMON GRAYSON, who joined City from Leeds: "I think there was a realisation that if we didn't get our act together, then we'd be in trouble and could go down. We didn't play well that day, in fact it was probably the poorest of that season. I wouldn't say there was panic but it's not nice being in that position. Obviously it's even worse when you're even lower than that."

KASEY KELLER: "Whenever we seemed to be in trouble in terms of a bad run of results, we always managed to turn it round with a couple of back-to-back wins. It was the same after that defeat at Leeds. We are a team that don't concede many goals, and if you're tight at the back you're always in with a chance."

MUZZY IZZET: "We knew that we were in a bit of trouble but we believed in our own ability and we felt that we were going to stay up. And we proved everyone wrong by being good enough to keep our Premiership place. Obviously when you're fifth from bottom, you start wondering that it might all go wrong, but we turned it right round."

COCA-COLA CUP QUARTER-FINAL AT IPSWICH

NEIL LENNON: "That was a great night. We beat Man United and thought 'We've got a bit of a chance' after getting drawn at Ipswich. I've never seen the gaffer so nervous before a game, he was pacing up and down the changing rooms. He said: 'Look lads, I'm as nervous as you, but we could really do with a result here'. I'd just broken my toe and was having injections but their doctor wouldn't give me one because it would do the toe more harm than good. Next thing, the gaffer came in and said: 'You better do this injection or I'll do it myself'. So yes, I did play!"

KASEY KELLER, a Cup giantkiller with Millwall: "We knew we had a good opportunity once we were drawn against a team from a lower division. We went there, did enough to get the win and on we went."

SHEARER'S ONE-MAN CRUSADE AT NEWCASTLE – FEBRUARY '97

NEIL LENNON: "One of the best moments of that season was when we went 3-1 up and Emile scored that goal. We just went through so many emotions. Even at 3-3

January 1998: Manchester United 0 Leicester City 1 (Cottee)
FANTASTIC!

we still couldn't believe it but, you know, a point's a point, right? For them to score in the last seconds was hell. We were dead on our feet completely. It was very cruel because we had contributed so much to the game, but Alan Shearer left us devastated with that hat-trick."

MUZZY IZZET: "We've come a long way to be able to go to Newcastle and dominate them so much that we're 3-1 up with 13 minutes to go. Alright, we did lose the game 4-3 but we did deserve something out of the game. We showed other teams in the Premiership that we can compete. Afterwards, the manager couldn't fault our commitment and the way we worked but you could see how disappointed he was."

MATT ELLIOTT, who scored at St. James' Park: "It was just silence in the dressing room afterwards. We were flabbergasted. It was down to Alan Shearer 100%, he was unstoppable getting three goals out of nowhere."

CHELSEA – THE FA CUP – AND THAT PENALTY

STEVE WALSH: "That was one of the low points of the season. We wouldn't have minded going out if they'd scored a 30 yarder in the top corner but to a decision like that, it really hurt us quite deep and that's why I was so pleased we beat them (2-0 in February 1998). It was so important to me. We really, really wanted to beat them. It's the same when we play Derby, we desperately want to win.

"After defending so well and causing them problems at Stamford Bridge, it was a great shame to go out in that way. He (O'Neill) was very hurt that by that. If I can remember right he didn't speak for a long time afterwards. It was such a horrible thing to happen"

SIMON GRAYSON: "I remember the gaffer in the dressing room and there was such a feeling of disappointment. To lose to a controversial decision like that is dreadful but referees do make mistakes, they can't always get it right. Obviously on the night it wasn't the right decision. If we'd got through that round anything could have happened. We would have been in the last eight of the FA Cup, an away trip to Portsmouth, but it just wasn't to be. At least we had a chance to get to Wembley via the League Cup."

BILL ANDERSON: "Martin O'Neill was very, very, very clever after this match. He said it was a disgrace, he said it was a disgraceful decision but at no time did he say Mike Reed had been a disgrace. He didn't personalise it. We knew what he was thinking but he never actually said it. That is why the FA couldn't charge him with anything. He chose his words very carefully which is quite a mental exercise in the heat of the moment. It wasn't a disgraceful decision . . . it was a scandalous decision. Dermot Gallagher was banned for one game for a poor FA Cup tie earlier this year, Mike Reed should never have been allowed to referee another game as long as he lives. If they'd lost to a 30-yard blinder or they might have lost the shoot-out, fair enough, Martin could have accepted that but the way it happened really rankled with him.

"A certain referee of my acquaintance who knows Mike Reed told me he nearly kicked the television in when the decision was made, and then said he wasn't surprised he gave it."

NEIL LENNON, who only played in the replay: "We felt robbed. They'd started to get on top but you expect that with them being the home side. It didn't look like we were going to win it in extra time so we thought we'd have a go with penalties. For the game to finish the way it did was a farce. Referees live and die on decisions like that but we always feel at Leicester that we don't get the rub of the green like the bigger clubs do."

MATT ELLIOTT, who was adjudged to have 'fouled' Johnsen for the penalty: "People still talk about it, don't they? If we had won that game we would have been in the quarter-finals and in the form we were in, who knows what might have happened. We battled away and felt we deserved to be in the shoot-out, but to be robbed in that manner was a big blow. To a certain extent I feel let down that a fellow professional could do that but it's fairly common nowadays. He dived past me into Spencer Prior and we thought at worst it was obstruction, so an indirect free kick. But he said it was for a foul on me! It was a sickener because the ref was in a good position to see it. The media interest it attracted afterwards was amazing."

KASEY KELLER: "We fought hard but even though they were the better team on the night, we were looking forward to the dice roll with the shoot-out. The player took a dive and the referee had a bad angle, made the call and that was that - a bad decision. Funnily enough, when I was at Millwall we beat Chelsea in the FA Cup on penalties! It would have been fun to see if I could have done it again."

MUZZY IZZET, a former Chelsea player: "It was a close, tight game and it was Erland Johnsen brought down for the penalty but I couldn't tell at that split second whether it was or not. On the action replay it was never a penalty, and that was a low point."

BILL ANDERSON: "Martin had, in many ways, this 'small club-big club' chip on his shoulder having made the team over-achieve in many peoples' eyes. He knew the team had no right to be on the same pitch with a side like Chelsea, of that stature at that time. He felt cheated in the football sense more than anything else, not personally, but just the fact that that team had, to coin a cliche, trained all week, the manager has coached all week, and you get something like that and there's nothing you can do."

COCA-COLA CUP SEMI-FINAL V WIMBLEDON

NEIL LENNON: "We didn't need firing up for this one. We were two games away from Wembley and I missed the first game which we should have won comfortably. In the second leg, they blitzed us for, like, 20 minutes in the first half and scored their goal. We weathered the rest of the storm and came out after the break in better shape. Larry (Simon Grayson) just shut his eyes and his header went in. It's not like him to do that! That was a brilliant night, we were so delighted."

Hard-working, ball-winning, tough-tackling, butt-kicking midfield ace –
Neil 'The Chief' Lennon

SIMON GRAYSON: "The first leg was a close game, there wasn't many chances, it ended nil-nil, and everyone had Wimbledon down as favourites. They presumably felt that Wimbledon would turn us over on their own patch and that would be it. Once again, and I make no apologies for repeating myself, you should never write Leicester off."

NEVILLE FOULGER: "Getting to the Final was no mean achievement when you consider they had to get past Wimbledon in the semi's. They're probably the team you would least want to play in a cup semi-final home and away. And who would have thought that Simon Grayson would be their goalscoring hero?"

MUZZY IZZET: "The second leg was similar to the Watford game the previous season because we took loads of fans to London for the match. The amount of support we had and the atmosphere was first class. Simon Grayson just popped up and got us through. It was a brilliant night. You don't really need extra motivation for a game like this. Once you step out on the pitch, you've got that many Leicester supporters there and they do it for you."

KASEY KELLER: "We were disappointed not to win the first leg, even though we didn't create a lot of chances. They didn't get the away goal which was crucial. Then they got a deflected goal in the return and we battled back to equalise. After that, it was a case of just fending them off as they came at us. Around this time, I was flying back and forth to the United States so it was very busy and exciting."

STEVE WALSH: "After the first game, I thought we deserved to be about 3-1 up. We drew nil-nil and we knew what to expect in the second leg. Nobody let us down. Simon (Grayson) scored a rare goal, and once we'd got that we felt we would win it."

SIMON GRAYSON, City's unlikely goalscoring hero . . . with his head!: "We went 1-0 down and I managed to get us back in it in the second half. It's not very often I score, and even less often that I score a header! It was just one of those games where we battled away, and played really well, and it was just a great team performance. We showed the determination, character and spirit to hold out against a team like Wimbledon who are noted for their team spirit. A great night all round."

COCA-COLA CUP FINAL and REPLAY v MIDDLESBROUGH

STEVE WALSH: "Leading the team out at Wembley went just one better than leading out the team on play-off final day. It was a big thing, it was a major trophy and it got us into Europe. It's something that everybody will always remember."

BILL ANDERSON: "The Coca-Cola Cup side was not the same one that was doing so well in the Premiership. Three players were cup-tied . . . Marshall, Guppy and Elliott. Co-incidentally Mark Robins came in for Marshall at Ipswich and scored the winning goal. Robert Ullathorne had come in and would have filled Guppy's place but got injured straightaway. So the achievement was not so much that they got to the final and won it but they did it without a full strength side. That's how it looked at Wembley. For me, when Ravanelli scored, that was the first time watching a Martin O'Neill side that I didn't think they had it in them to come back. Fortunately for Leicester City I was wrong. I just thought it was one game too far. Once Emile equalised and the final whistle went, I absolutely knew they would win the replay, and I think they did too."

PONTUS KAAMARK: "Both me and Mike Whitlow had been out for sometime and we were included. It wasn't really a gamble because I had been out with a broken arm so my fitness was alright. Me and Whits had been training a lot together, playing badminton, lots of running and I was just delighted to be playing. I was really scared as well, really nervous, because I knew the Swedish national coach was watching me on TV and that was a chance for me to impress him. There was a lot of things at stake for me and luckily the result was okay at Wembley."

NEVILLE FOULGER, who watched the Wembley final on TV while recovering from heart surgery: "It was a very, very poor match. As a neutral, you would regard it as very disappointing. But for City it finished up great with that goal right at the end from Emile Heskey."

SIMON GRAYSON: "Middlesbrough were always going to be classed as favourites because it was a big game and they had all the big international names like Ravanelli, Emerson and Juninho. We were seen as the underdogs because we had better than average players with a great team spirit. There was nothing flashy about us. It was a really disappointing game, you don't go there just for the occasion but again we fought back from being one goal down and to get the late equaliser was a big boost for us."

KASEY KELLER: "Wembley was just another game to be honest. I've played in better stadiums with bigger crowds. I didn't grow up watching Cup finals so it was like a big international for me. In all honesty, I thought the atmosphere at the replay was much better."

MUZZY IZZET: "In the space of a year, I'd gone from Chelsea's reserves to Premiership regular with two Wembley appearances thrown in. You're playing against the likes of Juninho, Emerson, Ravanelli . . . and that's what you want as a footballer, to play against the best."

NEIL LENNON: "We got tanked by Middlesbrough 3-1 the weekend after we qualified for the Final. At half time we were 3-0 down, and the gaffer said 'Right, I don't want that to happen again'. Juninho ran us ragged so we decided to put Pontus on him. What we didn't want to do was concede an early goal so we flooded midfield and sometimes we left Claridge up on his own. The game itself at Wembley wasn't a classic."

STEVE WALSH: "It was a brilliant day even at Wembley, we fought very hard and I suppose Middlesbrough had the better chances but didn't take them. We created our own chances to get back in the game, put them under a lot of pressure and ended up earning a replay, which we deserved in the end."

PONTUS KAAMARK: "Even though I've played in many big games, this was the first time I'd played at Wembley and it is like Mecca for us in Sweden. There is something special about Wembley. When you're 10 years old in Sweden and you go out playing football, you always imagine it's at Wembley, and there's a penalty in the last minute. It's just a fantastic arena and it was brilliant with all the Leicester and Middlesbrough fans."

NEIL LENNON: "When they scored we looked dead on our feet and I thought the game might peter out with a 1-0 win for them. Then we stuck big Walshie up front and Mark Robins came on and it made a difference. Heskey's late goal lifted us for the replay. We knew we could play better and we knew they couldn't. They were going through FA Cup matches against Chesterfield at the time and were fighting relegation with a fixture pile-up. We thought that would help us."

MATT ELLIOTT, who was Coca-Cola Cup-tied so had to sit out the final and replay: "I'd rather be here and miss out than not be here at all. I knew when I signed what the situation was....we could have gone out in the next round but as it was we won the cup. It was brilliant just to be at a club that had done so well. I felt really sorry for Ian Marshall who signed for us the day after the first round I think. Perhaps there's something there to be looked at. Maybe if your previous club is out you should be eligible to play. It wasn't all bad though - I got a free suit out of it!! And then there were the celebrations as well . . ."

DAVID NEILSON, whose filming commitments with Coronation Street DID allow him this time to sample Coca-Cola glory: "I went to Wembley and the replay and wasn't it fantastic? I've been to Wembley so many times over the years and with us losing the first few times, I sort of got used to accepting the feeling of defeat. You know, three days of feeling awful. When we won, I wasn't sure quite what to do. I looked across to the Middlesbrough section and all their fans had gone apart from three or four who just stood there watching the Cup being paraded. I knew exactly how they were feeling."

MUZZY IZZET: "It didn't make a difference winning at Hillsborough rather than at Wembley. The atmosphere, I would say, was even better in the replay because the crowd was closer. One of the best days of my life, really. To win a major trophy was unbelievable."

STEVE WALSH, named Man-of-the-Match in the replay: "On the night at Hillsborough, we were the better team. It took me quite a while for everything to really sink in. I was absolutely knackered but I tried not to show it. There was great emotion, it was such a great feeling and eventually when it all settled down, it really sunk in what we'd done."

PONTUS KAAMARK: "It's probably the biggest football achievement in my life. It was similar to the World Cup because when we got home to Sweden, the greeting was amazing. They're probably on a par."

SIMON GRAYSON: "The atmosphere for the replay was one of the best that you can be involved in. For Claridge to pop up with the winner again was unbelievable."

NEIL LENNON: "We changed our tactics a bit for the replay. They stuck me on the left hand side to just open up the game a little bit more and it worked. I thought we deserved to win at Hillsborough because we played really well. When we did score, we nearly conceded straight away but Kasey kept us in it. I just knew it was going to be our night when that happened. I remember the gaffer saying he would take the team into Europe, but it was fairly tongue-in-cheek, and then he did it. Fantastic."

KASEY KELLER: "I was delighted, obviously, with the replay result but of more concern was getting my ass down to Heathrow for a 7am flight the next morning! That was tough . . ."

NEVILLE FOULGER, back on Radio Leicester for the replay: "I wouldn't say it was one of the great games but it was much better than Wembley. Claridge turned up trumps again and got all the headlines but for me one of the heroes of both matches was Pontus Kaamark. The job he did on Juninho was terrific. I think it was beyond everybody's belief that they'd win a trophy. As for Claridge, he's part of Leicester's folklore now, isn't he?"

BILL ANDERSON, who has covered City matches for the Leicester Mercury for many years: "The atmosphere around the place was fantastic, especially amongst the Leicester contingent, who roared them on from beginning to end. I would have to say that Claridge's goal was the biggest moment for the club since I've been working here."

PONTUS KAAMARK: "That night we were all very happy and I think the fans certainly deserved it. This was one of the few games where the manager didn't have to motivate us that much because everything around it, like the build up, was almost enough. He said a few things to us about being mentally right. We just went out and played for our lives really.

"We wanted to win. We knew we had a chance and the pressure was really on them after we came back in the last minute at Wembley. It just felt right from the beginning. It was fantastic."

STAYING UP IN 1997

NEIL LENNON: "The West Ham game near the end was a real relegation scrap. They scored a messy goal and it summed up the night. Then we outplayed Man United and got a draw, then beat Sheffield Wednesday and Blackburn to secure our Premiership place. I'm still not quite sure how we ended up finishing ninth!"

Steve Walsh: A winner in every sense of the word.

SIMON GRAYSON, who won the fans' Player of the Year award 96-97: "It was a nerve-wracking end to the season. Probably getting to the Coca-Cola Cup Final disrupted us a little bit because we had one eye on that and our League form suffered. Once you do get into a rut of not winning games it's difficult to get out of. We felt we probably had enough points to stay up considering the teams below us were a bit adrift, the number of matches left and the likelihood of getting a win here or a draw there. But we didn't confirm our safety until the penultimate match against Sheffield Wednesday. There was a lot riding on it, a lot of pressure, everyone else was getting results and we managed to score a late goal to make it certain that we'd stay up. It was so tight at the bottom that with a few games left, quite a number of sides could mathematically have gone down. By winning the last two games we finished ninth and when you look at the end of season table, it's hard to believe we were in any danger of getting relegated."

PONTUS KAAMARK: "Staying up was the big achievement for the club that season. Before the season, everyone said Leicester were going to fall out of the Premiership, and most people were more interested in who would go with us. I think we proved we were a really solid side. The whole squad and coaching staff really worked together to get us on track, and fight to stay up. We ended in ninth, which wasn't bad at all really."

STEVE WALSH: "I think after we won the Cup we thought we were safe in the league. That was the wrong thing to do because we got dragged back into a situation we didn't need to. When we were up against it, we stepped up the pace again and finished ninth. I think we switched off when we won the Cup and in hindsight, that was a mistake."

MATT ELLIOTT, who scored the goal against Sheffield Wednesday to ensure safety: "It slipped by us really and we were back in the danger zone. I think the Cup win saw us relax subconsciously and it was touch and go for a bit. That night against Wednesday took a big weight off our shoulders. Martin O'Neill was quoted as saying it was more important than the Cup win. There was another good celebration as well!"

BILL ANDERSON: "Mathematically they weren't safe in the League until the penultimate match but so many things had to happen to see them relegated. He (O'Neill) was being professionally cautious. I never even considered relegation since Christmas anyway because of the results they were getting. Staying up was more important but winning the Cup was the bigger achievement, because of the team they had to use."

KASEY KELLER: "Winning the Cup was great but if we'd got relegated as well then the Coca-Cola success would have tasted sour. We slipped up a bit in the League and when we did beat Sheffield Wednesday, it was a lot of fun - a big celebration."

MUZZY IZZET: "Staying up was more important than winning the Cup. You want to be playing in the Premiership for Leicester City to progress as a club. You need to be playing top flight football. And if they'd said you get relegated and win the Cup, we wouldn't have took that. I wanted to stay up more than anything."

O'NEILL'S NEW CONTRACT – SUMMER 1997

PONTUS KAAMARK: "Even though I got signed by another manager, I consider him (O'Neill) the only one I've had. It's the first proper good manager Leicester have had for some time. Obviously people were delighted and the fans as well that he stayed. It's so easy when you're successful to jump on another ship, a bigger club, but he's stayed with us and that's been good."

MUZZY IZZET: "Once he committed himself to the club, the rest of the players thought 'We've got a good manager here' so we need to stick by him because he's done such a great job. And he's given the likes of me, Neil Lennon and the others a chance."

BILL ANDERSON: "I think it had to be a big thing for the club, not necessarily in football terms, but similar to Kevin Keegan at Newcastle where plans for the flotation had to show stability in key positions. And at any football club a key position is team manager. It was not a publicity stunt, but it had to be done for various reasons. The club didn't do themselves any harm too by publicly being seen to back him, even if privately some elements who never wanted him are still at the club. If anything went wrong, in my opinion, I think they would waste no time in moving in on him. Certain things behind the scenes lead me to that conclusion.

"I get the impression that Martin still feels unappreciated within Filbert Street, including the boardroom. And there's a lack of realisation and credit given to what he has done. Martin doesn't appear to have benefitted from the flotation considering it was his and the players' efforts to make the whole thing possible, I think he has every right to feel a bit annoyed at this. He seems to be under constant surveillance to justify himself, which I don't think he should be. In other words, people seem to be taking more out of his efforts than he is."

DAVID NEILSON: "Martin has done a terrific job, and I just hope the club are ambitious enough to keep him. I know he signed a new deal in the summer of 1997 but what are contracts nowadays? We're now going to move grounds, they built that fantastic Carling Stand, but we should have thought about relocating years ago. I just hope the Board give the guy the support he needs. He's a winner. He's going to win European trophies and I just hope it's with us."

CITY'S WONDERFUL START TO THE 97-98 SEASON

STEVE WALSH: "After beating Villa and Liverpool and drawing with Manchester United, we felt we could do something against Arsenal. It was a game we could have easily lost. In the end we got a point but it was a backs against the wall job. We were behind twice and came back from an almost impossible situation. Obviously I scored the second equaliser to make it 3-3 and then everything happened. Ian Wright had a go at me after the final whistle and I said 'Come on then, if you want to have a go, let's do it' kind of thing. It was as simple as that really. It was nothing that bad really and that's it, end of story. Apart from that, it was a great game for us and an exciting game for the crowd."

NEIL LENNON: "The expectation has been a lot higher this season because of the success we had last year. To be fair, we've done really well. It was probably the best time to play Villa, Liverpool, United and Arsenal before they got into their stride. We've done that again at the start of this year (1998), drawing at Villa, drawing with Liverpool and beating United, plus we beat Leeds and Chelsea."

KASEY KELLER: "The first win against Villa was big, then we went to Liverpool hoping to get a point like the previous year and we got three. We should have beaten Man United at home, and it was a bonus to draw with Arsenal. The fifth game at Sheffield Wednesday was disappointing as we were expected to win that."

MATT ELLIOTT, who scored twice in the opening four games: "To be unbeaten against four teams that were tipped for the title was amazing. A few people casted doubts again and thought we might struggle again but that probably fired us up a bit. We didn't want to be seen as one-season wonders."

ROBBIE SAVAGE: "We got eight points from our first four games when we'd have been happy getting four because of the standard of opposition. You can't be bad players to get results like we do. Take for example the four matches against Manchester United and Liverpool this season (97-98). We won both away games and drew at home, and that's not bad."

MUZZY IZZET: "We do well against the bigger clubs for some reason. We've played Manchester United twice this season and taken four points off them, the same for Liverpool. I think we've come on a long way this season from last season. Alright, we're out of the Cups but we're much more consistent in the league."

NEIL LENNON, much enjoyed the 3-3 draw with Arsenal: "We just don't know when we're beat. We never give up. You look at the characters in the team, it's great. Everyone goes on about the spirit but people don't realise that we are a good team, good individual players, a very talented bunch of lads. We work very hard for each other and that's why we've been so successful."

SEPTEMBER 20TH – CITY IN 3RD PLACE AFTER BEATING LEEDS

STEVE WALSH, who scored the winner at Leeds: "It's the highest position I've been with Leicester in 10 or 11 years. We were going very well there's no doubt. We would never have thought we'd be up there considering the opening fixtures to the season but it was very important that we got those points because we had a bit of a sticky spell before Christmas."

PONTUS KAAMARK: "When I looked at the start of the season, I thought 'oh God' because we could have been playing for a month, or four games, without any points. that was a fear that I had. It got our confidence right straight away. Suddenly, after seven games, we were joint second, or third on goal difference. That was unbelievable."

Our Father, who art in Heaven, Martin be thy name . . .

U.E.F.A. CUP AGAINST MADRID – AND *THAT* REFEREE

STEVE WALSH, who captained the team in Spain: "It was unbelievable. I've never been involved in anything like that before. It was great to get a chance like that late in my career. We took the game to them, a lot of people thought they were going to hammer us, but we went out there and put on a performance that was typical of one of Martin O'Neill's teams. We played very well, we could have had more goals early on, then we were under pressure and we felt that the penalty decision over there was tough on us."

MUZZY IZZET: "The gaffer and John Robertson told us that the referee would see things differently to those here, and the atmosphere would be totally different. They were right of course. Basically they told us to go out there and keep our mouths shut and just play fair. We worked hard for each other, lost 2-1, but didn't disgrace ourselves."

NEIL LENNON: "Those games were brilliant. To go to Madrid and go 1-0 up was brilliant - probably the highlight of the season so far, apart from beating Man United I suppose. In the second leg, we were on top until Garry was dismissed. As for the referee, well, even UEFA weren't impressed."

PONTUS KAAMARK: "I remember the home game (the second leg) most. That game was stolen from us. We were robbed. You should never really complain about referees but we had decisions against us and you need to have some luck with you. Juninho (who Kaamark man-marked in the Coca-Cup Final and replay, and both these matches) got his revenge so I wasn't happy about that at all. It was a really good team that we played against but nothing went with us so that was really sad. You can't do more than your best and that's what we did. Maybe we'll get there again."

STEVE WALSH, missed the second leg due to injury: "I couldn't believe it. I watched it from the stands and when their guy got sent off it we were just getting at them and looked like we were going to score. Then Garry Parker got sent off and it changed the whole complex of the game. If he'd stayed on, we'd have won that game. The referee was then banned from being in charge of any more UEFA Cup matches this season. That says it all."

MATT ELLIOTT, who captained City in Walsh's absence in the return: "It brought back memories when I watched Villa play over there on TV recently. We got the early goal in Madrid and suddenly we thought we might be able to do something in the competition. It wasn't to be, though. Everyone knows the referee made some ridiculous decisions and he was eventually suspended by UEFA. That doesn't happen too often so you can read a lot into that. We left the competition with our heads held high."

KASEY KELLER: "I wish we'd beaten a team first before playing Madrid. The referee effectively cost us the match, no doubt about it. Very rarely do I criticise officials, and if it's a split second decision, like at Chelsea in the Cup when the guy conned him, they can easily makes mistakes. But this was different. Once Garry Parker was sent off, it changed everything."

BILL ANDERSON: "I think they were unlucky in the first leg, and cheated in the second. UEFA took action against the referee . . . if only the FA had taken similar action against Mike Reed, but that's another story. Martin's main frustration was that they hadn't been beaten fair and square. Had they drawn 0-0 and Madrid had gone through, that's fair enough, but again that wasn't the point. Europe, if we're being honest, was well down his list of priorities. He took the Brian Clough line that going into Europe should be, in a manner of speaking, a bit of fun."

ROBBIE SAVAGE, who came on as a second half substitute at Filbert Street: "I've played against foreign opposition for Wales so I'd had a little taste of the big time but this was a bit different. The referee was terrible, wasn't he? You can't say too much about refs though nowadays and at least one of those penalties should have been given, maybe two and possibly three. They had a penalty over there, which never was, so we were robbed, you can say."

MUZZY IZZET: "The second leg was disappointing because I felt that the sending off of Garry Parker was ridiculous and cost us the match. We were getting on top and playing well but that's football for you. The referee didn't see our penalty appeals the way we did."

COCA-COLA CUP HORROR AT GRIMSBY

STEVE WALSH: "Very disappointing. We didn't play at all well, we had a couple of players out, me and Julian Watts got injured, I broke my ribs there so it was a bad night overall, especially as we were the Cup holders. We want to forget that."

NEIL LENNON: "That was a bit of a stinker. I fancied a good run again and we just didn't play on the night. A bad one for us. It just didn't happen."

KASEY KELLER: "At the time, there was no place in Europe for the winners, we'd just come back from Spain, and there wasn't a whole lot of motivation involved. Grimsby just hammered us, clear and simple. They were the better team. I couldn't apologise more to Julian (Watts) after punching him when I went for the ball. It fell to one of their players, they scored but it was just one of those things."

MATT ELLIOTT: "We were cruising for an hour and didn't look in trouble, then they changed their tactics and went 4-3-3 and we couldn't cope with it. Once the first goal went in it was a catalogue of disasters. Then Kasey came out and whacked Julian, Walshie ended up breaking his ribs when he collided with the post, they got the second and we fell apart. Fair play to Grimsby though who weren't a bad side."

PONTUS KAAMARK: "I didn't play in this one - make a note of that please, Geoff! That was one of my biggest achievements, not playing in this game. Seriously though, it was sad to lose."

A DISAPPOINTING END TO 1997

PONTUS KAAMARK: "I don't think it was a lack of confidence. Every team goes through it. Take Manchester United for example. We beat them, so did other teams (in early '98). As soon as we think that we are doing alright, you relax just a little bit, perhaps mentally, but we can't afford to be like that, we have to be 100% in our heads. The other teams have so much class so we have to be properly motivated and up for it and we can beat any team. We don't have the biggest squad and that sometimes affects us."

ROBBIE SAVAGE: "We had a blip at the end of the year but even the best go through that as Man United have found. We lost to Everton and drew against Sheffield Wednesday and we were disappointed. However, it shows how far we've come because we feel now that they're the kind of games we should be winning."

WHO HAS BEEN CITY'S BEST OR MOST IMPORTANT SIGNING UNDER O'NEILL?

MUZZY IZZET: "I think when we needed a boost last season we signed Matt Elliott and he made a big difference for us. He came in and strengthened the defence, scored a few important goals for us, you know. But at the same time, I think Steve Claridge has done a brilliant job for us, even though this season has been a disappointment for him. You look at the goals he's got for us, you can never take that away from him, a lot of Leicester fans appreciate what he's done for the club."

NEIL LENNON: "It's very difficult to choose. You could say Claridge, Matty Elliott, Muzzy, there's so many. Me, Claridge, Julian Watts and Muzzy all came at the same time and that's when things started to turn round. Elliott came in and made a big impression, but you can say the same thing about Claridge. His goals turned the club on its head. The goal at Wembley is now in City folklore. People call him a talisman and he did it again in the Cup final. Matty came at a different time, he's a great player but you'd have to go back to the spring of '96 for your answers."

NEVILLE FOULGER: "A vital signing, no doubt, was Matt Elliott. A lot of the fans feel that Elliott was probably his best signing and certainly the timing was important. His arrival in January 1996 gave them a huge lift. I think Neil Lennon, for £750,000, is an absolute snip. And take Muzzy Izzet . . . when you think Martin signed him without any senior playing experience, well, it's fantastic. He cost a bit less than Lennon but I think he's been sensational. Claridge as well has to come into the equation - his goals, especially at Wembley and Hillsborough in the two finals, more than repaid the £1.2 million. You have to say that Martin hasn't made a bad signing. People went on about Ian Marshall when he joined, saying he was too old or too slow for the Premiership, but he's done ever so well, scoring goals AND playing brilliantly in defence.

"If I had to single out one, it'd have to be Matt Elliott because he's an outstanding player. But I do think that Lennon and Izzet are not far behind."

SIMON GRAYSON: "That's a tricky one to answer. At the time, when we bought Neil Lennon, he was a big influence to the team, he worked his socks off, he fitted in straightaway and showed a lot of determination. Obviously, Claridge came along and scored the goals which helped get us up. Then you've got Matt Elliott who's proved to be an outstanding and talented player in the Premiership, who looks like he's been playing there all his life. It's difficult to pick one out of the three but I would say that they were the three major signings."

KASEY KELLER: "He's very calculated in the signings he makes. Spencer (Prior) and me came in at the start of the season to add some backbone. When Walshie and Julian were getting knocks, he brought in Matt Elliott and he's done a remarkable job for us. Ian Marshall has scored some big goals for us, Steve Guppy has done some good stuff on the outside. He (O'Neill) is a bit slow to make the signings but he definitely doesn't waste his money. For the budget he works to - for both fees and salaries - he's done a terrific job."

PONTUS KAAMARK: "It's hard to take something away from the others by singling out one person. There have been lots of good signings that have done really well. Neil (Lennon), Muzzy (Izzet), Kasey (Keller) etc but perhaps Matt Elliott because he's a big character, a giant at the back, really good to play alongside. You can feel the other teams have trouble when he's playing. He's really a giant in our defence and a good defence gives confidence to the other players."

ROBBIE SAVAGE: "It's got to be Matt Elliott at the back, because of the stability he gives us. I think Muzzy Izzet and Neil Lennon in midfield, both have been great signings. For the money he paid, those three have been terrific."

BILL ANDERSON: "In terms of value Matt Elliott has been the signing of the century but the most important signing Martin O'Neill made, and he'll never better it, is Steve Claridge. Without Claridge, none of this would have ever happened. He scored the winning goal at Charlton the next game after Sheffield United so he turned that situation round. He scored the last gasp goal at Wembley to take them into the Premiership. And he scored the goal at Hillsborough that took them into Europe. He was the man whose goals made everything possible. It was a mutual thing; Without O'Neill, Claridge wouldn't have done that, and without Claridge, O'Neill wouldn't be there. I'm certain that had City not gone up, O'Neill wouldn't have been the manager the following season. However, the best signing Martin has made is Elliott in terms of ability and importance long-term."

City's unsung hero Ponus Kaamark. Man-marking a speciality!

PETER JONES: "I think time will probably prove that Elliott is the best signing, and the best value for money. From speaking to people in the game, I know a lot of clubs looked at him but were scared off by his price. The £1.6 million Martin paid has proved to be excellent judgement. I think the other one that stands out for me is Muzzy Izzet, where a player with no senior level experience is bought and looks outstanding. Someone had obviously done a great deal of homework and great credit to the manager for bringing him to Leicester. Great credit also to the player who has took to the Premier League like he's been playing there all his life."

DAVID NEILSON: "There's been a phenomenal crop of signings since he arrived. Claridge's right boot has got to be worth something and I do think at that point he made that team along with Izzet and Lennon who were fantastic. He gave the team something extra. When we signed him I had my doubts, I must confess, but he's been magnificent. He made the team tick so much. So I'd have to say Claridge although it seems unfair not to talk about Lennon, Izzet, Elliott and even Rob Savage at £400,000. He's going to be a really good player. I don't think we would have signed Matt Elliott if Steve Claridge hadn't propelled us into the Premiership. His signings have been brilliant so far, but I reckon he'll make even better ones."

STEVE WALSH: "I don't think I could say one player. You look at it and I could name five or six who he's bought and have been absolutely brilliant. You can't split anybody really. You've got Elliott, Izzet, Lennon, Keller; all these players have been absolutely phenomenal and they've really given this team a big boost, you know. They're quality players, and have proven themselves. It's hard to pick one that's better than anyone else."

NEVILLE FOULGER: "When you add together the cost of Elliott, Lennon, Izzet, Claridge, Keller, Guppy and Zagorakis (£6.7m) it's still less than Stan Collymore (£7m). I think you'd sooner have those seven in your starting line up than Stan Collymore."

MATT ELLIOTT: "I think Neil Lennon epitomises Leicester. He's very consistent, he does a great job for us, perhaps he could score more goals - I'm sure he'll hold his hands up and admit that! He's mister consistency - the Chief, or so he thinks! He works his socks off, he's quicker than most people think, he puts his foot in and he can certainly play a bit. In training he's the man to have on your side as he doesn't give it away a lot. He gets fired up, he gets the lads going a bit but he's one of many that has done well here."

ONCE PLAYERS LEAVE, DO THEY STILL CARE ABOUT THE CLUB?

SIMON GRAYSON: "Leicester's result is always the first one I look for after a Villa match. I had a good five or six years at the club and thoroughly enjoyed myself. Most of the time anyway! It was a big decision to leave but I still knock around with one or two of the lads, because they're my mates."

MOST IMPRESSIVE OR IMPORTANT PERFORMANCE SINCE DECEMBER 1995

STEVE WALSH: "It's a tricky one. You look at the games which were important at the time when we were getting towards the run-in to promotion in '96. We were outside the play-offs, there were Charlton and Crystal Palace, both away, they were two massive games for this club and everyone of us fought tooth and nail to get those wins. They stand out for me as they went a long way to getting us promoted."

NEVILLE FOULGER: "I agree with Steve. They were on a bad run and needed a boost and they got that at Palace and Charlton. They'd just lost to Sheffield United and I think it was important that they were away from home. Another two big games came against Stoke in the play offs. There was a lot of worry when they drew at home in the first leg, but they showed their fighting spirit to get them to Wembley. People said Stoke were in the driving seat ahead of the second leg, and maybe they were, however, you write City off at your peril under Martin O'Neill. I think the best result since O'Neill arrived was at Old Trafford this year when City won one-nil."

ROBBIE SAVAGE: "Tottenham at Filbert Street was great but so was the performance up at Old Trafford, especially the first half against United. Both of those were special."

KASEY KELLER: "I would say probably Spurs at home when we won 3-0. We absolutely destroyed them, they hardly had a shot on goal. It was a great team annihilation. You can look at the wins in the Cup final and away at Old Trafford, but the Spurs game was 100% domination."

MATT ELLIOTT: "The Tottenham match does stand out, even though they weren't playing that well at the time. Over 90 minutes we were at our very best."

O'NEILL – WHAT IS THE SECRET OF HIS SUCCESS?

PONTUS KAAMARK: "It has been said so many times before that he's a good motivator, but it's not only that. I think it's his amazing passion for the game. He really lives every moment. He gets the most angry when we lose, the most happy when we win, and his passion rubs off on the players. You know you really have to go out and perform for him, to stop him getting really angry! That's the way you want it to be. He's very intelligent about the game. He himself played and he can see things that sometimes we can't."

SIMON GRAYSON: "He seems to have the midas touch when it comes to signing players. He looked at Matt Elliott for quite a while before buying him, he goes into their backgrounds and he's very thoughtful about whether they'll fit in to the team. He won't spend money just for the sake of it."

MATT ELLIOTT: "For some reason he manages to get the very best out of all his players, I don't quite know how. Sometimes he'll criticise players to try and get them to react and give an 'I'll show you' attitude."

KASEY KELLER: "I think the secret to his success is knowing which player to buy that will do a job in the position he wants. I've known managers who have bought players and tried to change them. He's rarely on the training field, he speaks well and gets people motivated but I wouldn't exactly call him the ultimate motivator. There's no secret gameplan. He just gets players to do what they're best at. If he wanted me to play like Rene Higuita (eccentric South American goalkeeper), I can't do it. If you want a Rene Higuita, you go and buy Rene Higuita. If you want a hard-working midfielder that tracks back, fights for it and tackles, you don't buy David Ginola. You buy Neil Lennon."

ROBBIE SAVAGE: "I think it's his desire to win and the passion he has. I've seen him at half time before going mad if things aren't working. He has the respect of everyone. He just walks in the dressing room and even if there's loud music playing and everyone talking, there's silence when we see him. That proves how much respect he's got. The great team spirit comes from him. He's brilliant. I can't say a bad word about him."

NEIL LENNON: "I think he's a great man. It's alright having the passion but you need the intelligence to go with it and that's what he's got. It's alright ranting and raving on the touchline but when he does it he has a meaning to it. His team talks last a minute. The way he looks at it is that if he gives you a 15 minute team talk, you'll forget 14 minutes of it, and remember the last one. He keeps it nice and short, and when he says something, it registers with you. That's what he's good at. And he says different things for different games.

"What he's done in the game for a start commands respect. His managerial record is brilliant, but he gets that respect because of the way he is. He takes it personally if we lose and that's a sign of how much it means to him."

DAVID NEILSON: "He's just so talented at his job. He's got a tremendous knowledge of the game and when you see him on matchdays he is so energetic. I hope he doesn't burn out. He chooses the right people to buy, because signing 11 good players doesn't guarantee a good 'team' on the pitch. I only met him once but he made a big impression on me. I'm just an actor so I was surprised when he was asking me questions . . . what about this, what about that . . . and his brain seemed to be going at 300 miles per hour!"

STEVE WALSH, City's most senior player: "He's got his own unique way of doing things. There's nobody like him, there's no doubt about that. But you've got to look at him and hold your hand up and say 'well done' because of the signings for one. He can spot a player. He knows how to get results, he's really proved that. Not everybody always likes the way he works but he knows what he's doing. He's signed some top class players and is turning them into international players. You've got to look at that and think 'hold on a minute' he's doing well. The scouting system isn't probably as good as some other clubs but he seems to rustle up these players from somewhere, which is very impressive."

PETER JONES, Leicestershire's top referee who is unable to officiate at City games: "I've met Martin a few times and I'm always made welcome by him, the coaching staff, players or office staff, and for that I'm both grateful and fortunate. Martin is the catalyst, he's a very shrewd operator and an excellent manager. I think the secret of his success is that he's very knowledgeable. I think he's a very good tactician and I think he's got a skill which is not easy to come by and that's getting the best out of players. You can see that because the players appear never ever to give up in any match. That's great credit to the manager."

BILL ANDERSON: "I think he's got an understated knowledge of the game. He undersells himself. He's not really made a bad signing, you could say. It took him 18 months to track Matt Elliott. He doesn't jump in for players, and Steve Guppy has been on his mind ever since he sold him from Wycombe to Newcastle. His knowledge of what players can do when fitted into the team is fantastic. Elliott's debut was against Wimbledon, the roughest, toughest, meanest bunch of attackers you could face in the Premiership and Leicester kept a clean sheet. Martin never sits in the stand, he's always right there by the pitch kicking every ball, living every moment and I think the players respond to that. In the early days it took a while to get across to the players that he was on their side. His touchline antics were a little bit disconcerting to the players at first but they've got used to it now. If they saw him totally motionless on the sidelines they would probably think: 'Christ, we are playing badly'."

MUZZY IZZET: "All his signings have been spot on. I think he can see a bargain. He doesn't complicate things when it comes to set pieces and tactics. He doesn't put too much information into your head. He just basically tells you to go out and work hard as a team. As long as every player in the team is doing it, you're going to get results. The team spirit here is as good as anywhere. When I was at Chelsea, it was a bit difficult because players lived all over the place. Here, when we do decide to go out, we go out together. Everyone gets on well. I think you can see it both on and off the pitch."

NEVILLE FOULGER: "I think he is a great motivator. His own enthusiasm, which is there for all to see on the touchline, spreads to the players. I think they've come to understand that he loves winning and hates losing, and he gives them enormous confidence. But I think he's got this touch of Brian Clough about him, a bit of magic you can't really put your finger on. People talk about Wimbledon, but I've never seen players work as hard as Leicester do. And that is down to Martin O'Neill."

MATT ELLIOTT: "The new Brian Clough? I don't know because I never played for him but I would imagine he has similar quirks. Both Martin O'Neill and John Robertson often harp on about Clough and the old times, ways he used to treat people, so I think they've picked up a bit from his style of management."

SIMON GRAYSON: "His passion for football in general and his passion to win is quite something. He hates losing and you just have to watch him on television to see the enthusiasm and passion he shows towards the team, it just rubs off on everybody else. When fans see someone as enthusiastic as that, they can associate with them so much more. He's a good motivator in the dressing room, he gets everyone going, he knows how to get the best out of them. He's also got some good assistants that help him, they make a good team."

BILL ANDERSON: "I don't think there are shades of Cloughie in Martin O'Neill. I think he learned some football things from Cloughie but his man-management appears to be quite different. It seemed he terrorised players into performing. That doesn't sound like the Martin I know. The only parallel I can draw is that in his first season he used to have the same green sweatshirt as Brian Clough!"

STEVE WALSH: "The dressing room is a happier place now than when he arrived but to be fair to him it was a difficult situation then. I think the whole adjustment thing to his ways was hard for everybody but we ended up very close as a team. You have the odd fight and moan and things but overall we've all come through it together and got on with the job.

"We hope he'll stay but that's something we'll find out in the next few years. We'll have to see how far he can take us. He's taken us a long way already and even if we slumped now, you have to say he's done brilliant. That would be a travesty if it did happen, of course. We need the backing to go on from here, and I'm sure we'll have more success if he stays."

Martin O'Neill and John Robertson: The new Clough and Taylor?

AND FINALLY, THE AUTHOR WOULD LIKE TO ADD . . .

In his first two years in charge, Martin O'Neill transformed Leicester City into a powerful outfit capable of holding their own in the top flight. He did it, too, on a limited budget and proved that even though he can't shop at Harrods, he can still find little gems in the bargain basement of his local corner shop. You can't really fault any of his signings; some have been better than others of course. But considering the money he paid for them, he's performed a miracle. Those new players enabled O'Neill to complete all the objectives (and more) that he set out on day one of his reign at Filbert Street.

After the debacle against Sheffield United, he rallied the troops and they responded by getting to Wembley and winning promotion via the play-offs. Ninth place in the Premiership was beyond everyone's wildest dreams, as was the Coca Cola Cup run which culminated in a fantastic night at Hillsborough. Promotion, a major trophy, consolidation in the Premiership, qualification for Europe, the list goes on.

He will leave one day, for bigger and better things. But supporters are clinging to the hope that that is well into the future. Don't be too sure. One thing which may accelerate his departure is the club's overall ambition. Cracks have appeared between the football side and the commercial operation at Filbert Street and that doesn't impress O'Neill. That divide could get wider and wider as the money men get a greater say. To be fair, this is probably the case at many other clubs as well.

The flotation, which has not been the success the club had hoped for, doesn't appear to have greatly benefitted O'Neill financially. There was talk of £12 million being put aside for new players. Either he's got it and hasn't spent it, or, more likely, he was given a much smaller amount. If that's true, you can see why O'Neill feels frustrated. Just because, in a sense, he's 'overachieved' in terms of money spent and success gained, doesn't mean the club's money men should rest on their laurels. They need to be pro-active rather than reactive.

The Board of Directors would do well to tread carefully over the coming months and make sure they back O'Neill to the hilt. That means publicly as well as behind the scenes. They've taken a step in the right direction to keeping him happy by looking to leave Filbert Street and move to a bigger, purpose-built stadium. That shows there is some ambition in the Boardroom after all.

Fans thought they'd never get over losing Brian Little (Villa fans now know how we felt!). They thought the same after Mark McGhee left. Whether it's the Northern Ireland job, the holy grail of Nottingham Forest, or somewhere different, supporters must accept he will want a challenge away from Filbert Street in the future. It is up to the Board, and especially chairman Tom Smeaton, to make sure that day is a long way off as O'Neill, in my opinion, is their biggest asset.

To sum up, his first two years at Leicester were breathtaking. His passion and desire is refreshing. And he will go on, without doubt, to greater things. Let us hope he can manage that by staying with Leicester City.